THE CHINA DREAM: GUANGDONG STORY

中国梦·广东故事

DYNAMISM

活力的广东

XU JING

TRANSLATED BY LIU XI

SPM

Southern Publishing & Media Co.Ltd.
Guangdong People's Publishing House Ltd.

Editors: Lu Xuehua, Wu Mingxin
Published by Guangdong People's Publishing House Ltd., China
www.gdpph.com

First published 2017
Printed in the People's Republic of China

The China Dream: Guangdong Story-Dynamism/ Xu Jing and translated by Liu Xiaoxue
ISBN 978-7-218-11890-1 (paperback, 1st edition)

Preface

Located in southern China, Guangdong Province is the first region in China to implement the reform and opening up, and it is also one of the most affluent areas nationwide. The Pearl River, China's third largest river, runs across the whole province. The Pearl River Delta is an alluvial plain flushed by the Pearl River. After nearly 40 years of rapid development, it has already become one of the most important city groups of China. The Hong Kong Special Administrative Region, and the Macao Special Administrative Region adjoin to Guangdong Province. With the natural geographical relations and the same cultural background, they constitute China's unique Guangdong-Hong Kong-Macao Greater Bay Area—a world-class vigorous economic and cultural area.

For nearly 40 years of rapid development, Guangdong has been playing a leading role in innovation, spurring the rapid development of new growth drivers. There are many rapidly grown-up enterprises in Guangdong, such as Huawei, Tencent, and UMi, which have become important engines of Guangdong's new economy development. Huawei and Tencent are now widely known in China. We try to approach such enterprises and their employees, to find the "secret" of the most innovative and cutting–edge development in Guangdong.

Guangdong has been the most dynamic foreign trade area in China since ancient times. And Guangzhou has been a commercial city through the ages, as well as an important interconnecting city alongside the "Maritime Silk Road". Foreigners from all over the world travel across major cities in Guangdong everyday, sightseeing, attending business meetings, studying or visiting friends. In Guangzhou, there are a large number of foreigners from Europe, America, Southeast Asia, the Middle East, Africa and other places, doing business here everyday. They ship back clothing, fabric, seafood, electrical appliances or glasses; foreign trade is booming. In the Shenzhen Special Economic Zone ports, people and vehicles travelling between Hong Kong and Shenzhen are always lined up. Foreigners living here for many years gradually adopt and merge into customs and culture of Guangdong, and regard Guangdong as their "second home". Meanwhile, tens of millions of workers from other provinces live in Guangdong, especially in the Pearl River Delta, where they work in factories, earn money to support their families, and try to realize their own dreams and ambitions. Whether foreigners or migrant workers, they are all practitioners, promoters and witnesses of Guangdong's reform and opening up. We conduct close observation of their work and life to record their ups and downs.

Ten years ago, the per capita income in the Pearl River Delta had already reached the level of that of moderately developed countries, and it is moving towards high–income phase. But the embarrassment is that in the eastern, western and northern parts of Guangdong Province, there are still large number of underdeveloped rural areas, and some places are even in extreme poverty, which distresses successive provincial governments. The government is determined to carry out large–scale "poverty alleviation" action, and vows to lift all peasants of impoverished areas out of poverty in three years, and promote common prosperity in these parts of Guangdong like the Pearl River Delta.

As the most populated, dynamic, and developed province that has been spearheading reform and opening up, recent practices in Guangdong are full of strength and sweetness. We go into it, and hope to find and record those breathtaking, touching and impressive stories of the development in Guangdong these years. Those people and those stories constitute a glaring part in the glittering development of the new era in Guangdong.

Through these stories, you can see diligence and endeavors of Guangdong people in the process of modernization. Through the perspective of Guangdong, you can see great efforts of Chinese people in realizing the China dream of the great rejuvenation of the Chinese nation.

总序

广东省位于中国南部，是中国最早实行改革开放的区域，也是目前中国最富庶的地区之一。中国的第三大河流珠江穿越广东省全境，由珠江冲积而成的珠江三角洲在经过近40年迅速发展后，已经成为中国最重要的城市群之一。香港特别行政区、澳门特别行政区与广东省毗邻，天然的地缘和一脉相承的人文情缘，构成了中国独有的粤港澳大湾区——一个世界级活跃的经济人文区域。

和中国其他地区一样，在经过长达近40年的高速发展之后，广东面临产业转型升级转变发展动能的重任，创新驱动成为推动此轮变革的重要抓手。广东省内有许多近年来快速成长起来的新型企业，比如华为、腾讯、有米科技，它们成为广东新经济发展的重要引擎。华为和腾讯，以及它们的“老板”任正非和马化腾，在中国几乎家喻户晓。我们试图走近这样的企业及其员工，找到广东创新驱动最前沿的发展“密码”。

广东自古以来是中国对外商贸最活跃的地区，广州是千年商都，是“海上丝绸之路”重要的节点城市。来自世界各地的外国人每天往来于广东省内各大城市，他们或旅游观光，或商务会议，或求学访友。在广州，每天大量来自欧美、东南亚、中东和非洲等地的外国人在这里做生意，他们把这里的服装、布匹、海产品、电器或者眼镜托运回国，外贸做得红红火火。在深圳经济特区口岸，进出香港和深圳的车辆、人流常常排成长龙。长年生活在这里的外国人，在生活习俗和文化上逐渐接受并慢慢融入广东，广东成为他们的“第二故乡”。与此同时，更多的数千万计的来自中国内地的普通劳工常年生活在广东尤其是珠江三角洲地区，他们在工厂里“打工”，凭借“打工”挣下的钱养家糊口，并试图实现自己的人生梦想。无论是外国人还是农民工，他们都是广东改革开放的实践者、推动者和见证者。我们近距离观察他们的工作和生活，记录他们的喜怒哀乐。

珠江三角洲地区早在10年前人均收入便已达到中等发达国家水平，正迈向高收入阶段。但令人尴尬的是，在广东省的东、西、北部仍有大片生活并不富裕的农村，一些地方甚至还处于贫困状态，这让广东省历届政府颇感头痛。政府下决心开展大规模的“扶贫”行动，并发誓要在3年后让所有贫困地区的农民摆脱贫困，力促粤东西北地区与珠江三角洲地区走向共同富裕。

作为人口最多、经济最活跃、总量最大、地处改革开放前沿的省份，广东近年的实践既具有力量又让人感到温馨。我们深入其中，希望通过我们去发现去记录，在广东发展这些年中，那些或动人心魄或充满温情或饱含人性的故事。那些人，那些事，终将构成广东新时期史诗般发展历程中炫目的一环。

通过这些故事，人们可以看见，在现代化进程中广东人的奋发图景；透过广东，可以看见中国人民为实现中华民族伟大复兴的中国梦的奋斗历程。

Contents

Contents

目 录

目　录

Guangzhou: The Ancient Port Achieves New Developments

The Past and Present of Huangpu Ancient Port

In December 2015, Guangzhou, the provincial capital of Guangdong province, a metropolis with more than 13 million population, was holding the "Goteborg" porcelain exhibition in Guangzhou Museum. The nearly 100 pieces of porcelain set out from Guangzhou in 1745 but slept more than 200 years at the seabed of the Swedish port of Goteborg. In the words of the Chinese people, it is regarded as "back home".

On January 11, 1745, the Swedish merchant ship "Goteborg" went back home from Guangzhou. The ship was loaded with about 700 tons of Chinese goods purchased in Guangzhou, including 366 tons of tea, 500,000 to 700,000 porcelains, as well as silk, rattan articles and mother of pearl. It is the third time this ship came to Guangzhou, also the last time.

In 1757, the Qing government announced the implementation of "Canton System". The countries traded with China all needed to and could only come to Guangzhou.

That year, according to China's old calendar, was the 22nd

"Kang-Qian Flourishing Age", in which "Qian" refers to the Emperor Qianlong, is in Chinese history the heyday of culture, economy and handicraft industry. The picture shows the Emperor Qianlong.

year of Qianlong in Qing Dynasty. Qianlong was the reign-title of the imperator Aisin Giorro Hongli at that time. In ancient China, when the new emperor ascended the throne, a reign-title was set to calculate years to distinguish from the predecessor (mostly his own father). The 22nd year of Qianlong has been the year when Qianlong was on the throne for 22 years.

Qianlong means "Blessed Prosper and Flourishment", and the fact is the case. Qianlong, with a life span of 88 years, was the emperor who lived the longest in ancient China. The period, from his grandfather Emperor Kangxi (one of the ancient imperators who were most appreciated by Chinese) to his father Emperor Yongzheng to Emperor Qianlong, was the heyday of culture, economy and handicraft industry in Chinese history. In China, the greatest praise for a dynasty is named as flourishing age—maintaining prosperity in a long time—the three emperors created China's "Kang–Qian Flouring Age".

"Qian" in "Kang–Qian Flourishing Age" represents Emperor Qianlong. Qianlong claimed to be "The Shi Quan Old Man", with "Shi Quan" meaning perfect, from which the emperor's self–confidence is obviously seen. In China, he was also the one who wrote the largest number of ancient poems which were said to be more than 30,000, and even those great poets in the golden age of Tang Poem and Song Verse cannot be compared with him.

After 35 years' implementation of "Canton System", in 1792, Britain sent the fleet of Macartney to China in the name of making up for celebrating Qianlong's 80th birthday. According to the rules, vassal states needed to kneel when they saw the emperor. The two sides had controversies over whether to kneel or not and how to kneel on the matter of dignity and state system but in fact more of cultural gap. Later generations will hold the view that it is a symbol of China's change from openness to seclusion.

After sailing for 8 months, the "Goteborg" came to the sea about 900 meters away from the Port of Goteborg, and the crews who had been 30 months away from home could see their hometown. However, at that time, the bow hit the rocks and immediately sank. People who were waiting for triumphant return on the shore had to watch the ship sailing to the sea. Fortunately, all the crew were safe and sound.

About one–third of the goods were salvaged. These goods were sold on the market and unexpectedly made a profit of 14 percent in addition to pay the full cost of the trip to Guangzhou. The ship "Goteborg" and two–third of the goods were buried at the bottom of the sea, quietly waiting for

"Goteborg III" visited Guangzhou.

the moment more than 200 years later to once more see the light of day.

In 1984, a Swedish folk archeological activity found the wreckage of the ship "Goteborg". Two years later, archaeological excavations began. Soon, more than 400 pieces of complete porcelain and 9 tons of porcelain pieces were salvaged. Most of these porcelains were with traditional Chinese patterns, and a small amount of porcelains were painted with characteristic European patterns. Obviously, they were specially ordered by "Goteborg specially" for specific customers.

150 years later, in 2009, the "Goteborg" once again came to Guangzhou. However, this time it was a new ship built by imitation of the old ship. Chinese people habitually call it "Goteborg III".

It took craftsmen ten years and cost 30 million US dollars to build this ship.

To welcome the "new friends", Guangzhou spent a huge sum of money reconstructing two wharfs at Huangpu Ancient Port and Nanhai God Temple. The two piers and their surroundings are modeled on the ancient style, restoring the scene more than 200 years ago. They want to show Chinese marine culture represented by the maritime Silk Road, Guangzhou's history of trade, and reshape the reputation of the ancient port in the world.

The sailing route of "Goteborg III" was also arranged in accordance with the sailing route of "Goteborg", which is the longest sailing route in the world before the 16th century. Everything went well, but it spent more than 300 days coming to Guangzhou with a journey of 3700 km.

The Swedish king, Carl XVI Gustaf, and the Queen Sylvia arrived on the same ship. It is said that it is the king's own request to select Guangzhou as the first destination in China. Cantonese lived up to Swedish people's friendship, and visitors streamed into Guangzhou.

The new-sharp magazine *New Weekly* made a comment on this trip: two cities in two countries, with an archaistic sailing ship and an ancient business routes, performed a wonderful show with 200 years of historical connotations. CCTV recorded this pioneering work into the "Discovery" column, and Cantonese saw it as "an unaffordable great opportunity to promote Guangzhou". The Swedish turned the plan into a very creative "cultural image project". The renascence of "Goteborg" shows successful public relations, including marketing of sponsors, international trades and cultural exchanges.

"Goteborg III" is connected to the history and future of Guangzhou's foreign contacts. After arriving Guangzhou, as in 1857, it parked in Huangpu Ancient Port—a port which had never lost contact with the outside world for 1500 years and the only port which allowed for trading when the Seclusion Policy was carried out in the late Qing Dynasty.

"All foreign merchant ships importing foreign goods shall not berth along the river bay and must be anchored in Huangpu." Huangpu is Huangpu Ancient Port. Within the 80 years from 1758 to 1837, there were 5107 foreign merchant ships parking in the ancient port of Huangpu. As the only port in China for a long period, it witnessed the prosperity of "Maritime Silk Road" in Guangzhou. It also welcomed the U.S. merchant ship "Empress of China", the Russian "Hope" and other foreign merchant ships, especially the "Empress of China" whose visit to China opened the door of Sino–US trade.

The Memorial Archway of Huangpu Ancient Port.

The Chinese historian Huang Renyu pointed out in his book *A Year of No Significance* from a historical point of view that China's falling behind in the process of modernization was not due to moral and personal factors but the technological failure in achieving "mathematical management." But in some figures, in fact, Chinese people have done well. For example, about the statistics of the 5107 ships.

The great Chinese historian, litterateur and ideologist Sima Qian once wrote that Guangzhou is a metropolis "full of pearls, hawksbills, fruits and fabrics". Huangpu Ancient Port is located at Xingang East Road in Haizhu

That year merchant ships gathered on the Pearl River.

District in Guangzhou. Huangpu Village, where Huang Port locates in, keeps still the quaint scenery with a large banyan tree next to the ferry standing askew, shining banana trees and few fishing boats, without any traces of business.

The original name of Huangpu Village is "Fengpu". In the south of the village there stands a colorful memorial archway with two characters "Feng" and "Pu" on it near the Pearl River. As a legend goes, a pair of Phoenix flied into this place, after which the population increased and people had a bumper grain harvest. Legend will always be beautiful and auspicious.

The village locates in a small island. In China, the waterside area is called "Pu", and the land in water is "Zhou". So the village is named "Huangzhou" or "Fengpu", and then its name developed into "Huangpu".

A lot of historical sites and cultural relics kept by the village witness generational prosperities of the "Ancient Maritime Silk Road", prove the unique historical status of Huangpu Ancient Port, and reflect the great changes taking place in Guangzhou. Huangpu village is a living museum of "Ancient Maritime Silk Road", because the most valuable history exists in the hearts of people.

The prosperous development of Huangpu Ancient Port is in the 17th century to the 19th century when the

Huangpu Ancient Port.

development of the overseas trade in Guangzhou comes to its peak, that is, “the golden age of trade to China” which is what the modern Western businessmen often talks about. In 1769 the British man William Hick came to Guangzhou. He was full of praise for Guangzhou: “The scene of ships running on the Pearl River is like the Thames under London Bridge, and the differences between them lie in the different forms sailing boats on the river as well as galleons.” In the eyes of foreigners, nothing is more spectacular than the long array of sailing ships.

Some people made an evaluation like this: ships set sail from Huangpu Ancient Port in Guangzhou in the east seacoast, transport silk, porcelain, and tea to all parts of the world. At the same time, farming and handicraft technology, papermaking technology and compass were also taken to them. Monks, scientists, artists and translators who took the merchant ships back and forth are the messengers promoting cultural integration. In this sense, in the long history of thousands of years, as one of the birthplaces of the maritime Silk Road, Guangzhou is a starting point of the trip for Chinese civilization to have an influence on the world.

The old days have gone. The glory of the past gradually disappears in the gradually silted ferry of ancient port. And the pier is not busy and bustling as it was. History should be borne in mind. It is not a bad idea to build a historical museum of Huangpu Ancient Port, and Cantonese have done so.

One ancestral hall in the village is reconstructed into the historical museum of Huangpu Ancient Port. The area of 2000 square meters consists of three parts: the mural area, the area of material object and the central area. Among them, the area of material object is the most distinctive part of the museum. Designers gathered together more than 40 pieces of ancient building materials scattered in the ancient village of Huangpu, such as stone beams, stone pillars, stone carvings to create a scenic area of "Ruins" in the yard. They did not enclose these cultural relics to show them to visitors, because they hoped visitors could closely feel the glory of the culture of the ancient port.

In the mural area of the exhibition hall, there lies a large gilded mural made of white marble, with 31 meters in length and 15 meters in height. The painting portrays the prosperous scene of thousands of ships in Huangpu Ancient Port during the period when the "Canton System" was implemented. "Goteborg" and "Empress of China" are among them. This mural should be designed based on pictures left by some foreigners when they made sketches.

In Huangpu Ancient Port, an important seaport for foreign trade, many ships gather, economy prospers and the villagers also have early contact with foreigners and foreign cultures. Many villagers study abroad, engage in trade and become celebrities. For example, Hu Xuanze, the consul of Qing government, Japan and Russia in Singapore; Liang Cheng, the student who studied in America and reclaimed extra indemnities from the American president to construct Tsinghua University; Feng Zhaoxian, the one who delayed his disease for rescuing Sun Yat–sen, as well as the rail expert Hu Dongchao, the agricultural expert Feng Rui and the economist Liang Fangzhong.

In the Huangpu Village, there is a mysterious story about a Japanese wife who protects villagers from Japanese army invasion, which is quite legendary.

In 1900, Feng Zuoping, a villager in Huangpu Village, studied in Japan and met a Japanese girl. They soon got married. In 1924, because of homesickness and the need to attend upon parents, Feng Zuoping who was more than 40 years old came back to Huangpu Village from Japan with his families.

In order to release his wife's homesickness, Feng Zuoping built a small Japanese–style house for his wife, so that she could live in peace. This is the "Japanese House" now located at No.8, Dunyong Street in Huangpu Village.

After Japan launched the war of aggression, Guangzhou was occupied. A team of Japanese troops came to the Huangpu Village, and the villagers would soon be slaughtered. Suddenly, Feng Zuoping's wife appeared in front of the Japanese, showing a treasured sword. After Japanese troops saw the sword, they put their swords down, venerably worship the treasured sword, and then went out of the village. During the Anti–Japanese War, the Japanese army never invaded the village of Huangpu.

Villagers near the village got to know that the Japanese troops did not dare to enter Huangpu Village, they had to hide in the village of Huangpu. Therefore, Huangpu Village is also known as "Ping'an Village", with

"Ping'an" meaning "safe". In 1944, Feng Zuoping's wife died of illness and was buried on the top of the mountain inside Huangpu Village.

About the origin of the knife, in Huangpu Village there are three kinds of popular sayings. The first saying is that Feng Zuoping's wife is a remote relative of the Emperor of Japan. It is also said that she is a general's niece at the end of Japanese Shogunate period, and the sword is given by the general; one more saying is that she is a prime minister's niece, and the sword is given by the prime minister.

An old man who is familiar with the history of the village is more in favor of the third saying. "Japan is a hierarchical country. If she is from the royal family or the shogun's relative, she is impossible to marry an alien or a civilian." Anyhow, the Japanese wife makes great contributions to Huangpu Village.

Maintain Prosperous for 2000 Years

"Goteborg" did not make it when it would come home soon after going through difficulties. However, "Nanhai No.1", another ship which Chinese people are more familiar with, soon sank into the sea after leaving Quanzhou Port in China.

Quanzhou, another important port in ancient China, is one of the four major ports in the world in Tang Dynasty, the largest port in Song Dynasty and labelled by Marco Polo as "the Bright City". Marco Polo may be one of the few Italians who are more famous in China than in Italy. He described his experience in China in *The Travels of Marco Polo*, which aroused Europeans' enthusiastic longing for the Orient, and had a tremendous impact on the future discovery of new travel routes. However, many people doubt that his descriptions of China are sometimes slightly exaggerated.

Different from "Goteborg" which can only be imaged by future generations, "Nanhai No.1" who witnesses the history of Maritime Silk Road can show us his true appearance because of the complete evacuation.

In 1987, in Yangjiang, a sea area in the southern province of Guangdong, a shipwreck with a history of 800 years was found. It was later known as "Nanhai No.1" and is by far, among all discovered shipwrecks, the oldest, largest and most complete merchant ship for ocean trade in the world. It is estimated that it is 30.4 meters long, 9.8 meters wide, and the hull (not including the mast) is about 4 meters high. The displacement is more than 600 tons, and the dead weight capacity is about 800 tons. In fact, we do not know the name of this ship. Perhaps it has no name.

After "Nanhai No.1" was loaded at Quanzhou Port, probably due to storm or leak or some other unknown reasons, it finally sank into the sea. Exactly 20 years later, it was found and salvaged by creatively employing the plan of "raising integrally". The shipwrecks and cultural relics together with their surrounding water and silt were hoisted and transferred to the museum of "Maritime Silk Road" in Guangdong province, and then these cultural relics were sorted.

No one does not care about what is in the "Nanhai No.1". On January 15, 2016, a total of more than 14,000 sets of cultural relics and 2575 specimens were unearthed, among which there were more than 13,000 pieces of porcelain, 151 sets of gold, 124 sets of silver, 170 pieces

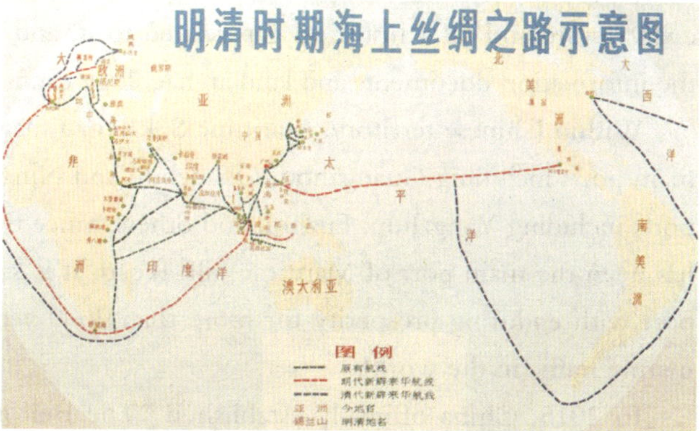

The Maritime Silk Road in the Ming and Qing Dynasties.

of bronze, about 17,000 coins and lots of animal and plant specimens, ship wood and so on.

"Nanhai No.1" is on the channel of the ancient Maritime Silk Road. Maritime Silk Road is the main artery of marine traffic connecting the East and West. Because the main bulk commodities are silk, it is named "Maritime Silk Road". As the goods transported changes, it has also been called "the maritime road of ceramics" and "the maritime road of spices". Starting from the southeast coast of China, through the Indochina Peninsula, the South China Sea countries and then the Indian Ocean, getting into the Red Sea, the ship arrived in East Africa and Europe. In the Song and Yuan Dynasties, China had a direct business contact through "Maritime Silk Road" with more than 60 countries in the world. The success of Zheng He's voyage in the Ming Dynasty indicated that Maritime Silk Road developed to its heyday.

Despite the prosperity, during quite a long period the Maritime Silk Road is only found in few documentary records, so people know little about it. Until in the 20th century when porcelain, silk and other cultural relics from China were found one after another at the ports along the route, Maritime Silk Road were gradually known to us. "Nanhai No.1" can provide a credible model for the study of this phase of history, and even restore and fill a historical gap related to it, and even more presents the information documents and land archaeology cannot provide.

Within Chinese territory, Maritime Silk Road mainly consists of three main ports including Guangzhou, Quanzhou and Ningbo as well as feeder ports including Yangzhou, Fuzhou and others. Since the 230s, Guangzhou has been the main port of Maritime Silk Road. It is known as only major port with enduring prosperity for more than 2000 years in the history of marine traffic in the world.

In 2015, China officially established "The Belt and Road" strategy (abbreviated as B&R) which is the abbreviation of the Silk Road Economic Belt and the 21st–Century Maritime Silk Road. It would fully rely on the existing double multilateral mechanism between China and relevant countries, with the existing and effective regional cooperation platform, borrow historical symbols of the ancient Silk Road, hold high the banner of peaceful development, actively develop economic partnership with the countries along the line, and create an interest community of political mutual trust, economic integration and cultural tolerance, a community with a common future and a community with common responsibility.

Guangzhou's "Stretching" Exercises

In the 19th century, the Sino-US trade was realized through transactions between commercial firms. There was a businessman named Wu Bingjian, whose firm had long enjoyed a good reputation in the United States and whose business almost monopolized the market. However, compared with his real name, the merchant Howqua was more well-known to American businessmen, and Hu-Kwa Tea is hence the name.

In 2014, Robert Forbes, the associate professor of the University of Connecticut and the director of the Forbes Museum, established the Forbes House Museum, the first Sino-American trade museum, in his ancestral home left by his ancestors in Milton, Boston. This museum, whose area is small, well preserved every item brought back by his ancestors from Guangzhou.

Robert Forbes' great-great-grandfather is also named Robert Forbes. At the age of 13, with all kinds of hardships, he came to Guangzhou by a merchant ship and went to his uncle who ran a firm to learn doing business. He kept close contact with Wu

Bingjian. When he left Guangzhou, Wu Bingjian gave him a self-portrait as a souvenir. It is in the process of listening to these past events, looking at these carefully preserved Chinese portraits and porcelain that Robert Forbes slowly grows up.

Wu Bingjian's father, Wu Guoying, had been engaged in foreign trade and set up the Ewo Hong in 1783. Wu Bingjian was born in 1769. At the age of 32, he took over the Ewo Hong, after which his family business grows up rapidly. At the age of 60, he and his family owned the property up to 26 million silver dollars. They not only owned real estate, house property, tea mountains, shops and huge sums of money in China, but also invested in railways, securities trading and insurance business in the United States. The Ewo Hong became a veritable multinational consortium.

The businessman Wu Bingjian in Qing Dynasty enjoyed a great popularity in the western business circles.

In 2001, the Wall Street Journal specifically made a list of the world's richest 50 people in the last 1000 years. Among them, there are six Chinese people, including Genghis Khan, Kublai Khan, Liu Jin, He Shen, Wu Bingjian and Tse–ven Soong. The Wall Street Journal made a comment like this. "Born in 1769, the Qing Dynasty Merchants Wu Bingjian, inherited his father's business, engaged in foreign trade, and further lent foreign merchants money and hereby obtained great wealth. He enjoyed a great popularity in the Western commercial circles."

Western businessmen considered Wu Bingjian to be "honest, cordial, careful, generous, and rich", and the British complimented him for his skill in financial management and extremely intelligence. It is said that Wu Bingjian adopted advanced business philosophy and established a close contact with important customers in Europe and the United States. As a widespread story goes, an American businessman was unable to pay off his debts of more than $ 70,000 to Wu Bingjian due to poor management. After Wu Bingjun learned of it, he tore up the receipt and announced the accounts were settled, so that the businessman could return to his home. Wu Bingjian knew well the importance of the "trademark". He attached his portrait to the tea sold overseas. Although this seemingly thin businessman did not leave Guangzhou throughout his life, his portrait went to the Americas, Britain and India with the goods.

The great businessman in the late Qing dynasty was once the richest man in the Thirteen–Trades Monopoly, and the Ewo Hong has also become the epitome of the development of the Thirteen–Trades Monopoly. The Thirteen–Trades Monopoly is the general term of the foreign–trade firms specially permitted by the government, not necessarily thirteen firms.

After the "Canton System" was carried out in Guangzhou, businessmen from the Thirteen–Trades Monopoly became the only

The trade in the Thirteen-Trades Monopoly in the Late Qing Dynasty in the 18th century.

housekeepers dealing with foreign affairs of the Qing Dynasty during more than 80 years. In addition to doing business, for foreign businessmen, things like sales of goods and their daily routines, whether important or trivial, must be handled by the Thirteen–Trades Monopoly.

However, after Treaty of Nanking provided for the opening of Guangzhou, Xiamen, Fuzhou, Ningbo and Shanghai as treaty ports (known as the "five–port trading"), the Thirteen–Trades Monopoly no longer had the exclusive monopoly of China's foreign trade. And the Thirteen–Trades Monopoly was declining.

The Thirteen–Trades Monopoly was once the commercial center of Guangzhou. The vicinity of the place where it is located, including the Beijing Road area has always been the administrative center of Guangzhou city, the center of Cantonese culture in modern China and the most prosperous commercial distribution center in the history of Guangzhou.

Until after the policy of reform and opening–up was implemented,

Zhujiang New Town, the CBD of Guangzhou city, is a symbol of the rapid development of Guangzhou. In the picture the two tallest buildings are respectively Guangzhou International Finance Centre and Chow Tai Fook Finance Centre (on the right). Below the picture is Haixinsha, the place where the opening ceremony of Guangzhou Asian Games was held, a small island in the Pearl River. Photographer: Liu Lei

the business district in the central old city area with the Beijing Road shopping district as the core and the business district along the central axes of the new city area with the Teemall as the core, became the dual power motivating the development of Guangzhou city and its economy together.

Guangzhou changes so fast. The change of city centers, from the city landmark, Nanfang Building, with a saying "One who fails to reach Nanfang Building does not actually come to Guangzhou", to the later Beijing Road Pedestrian Street, Tianhe Teemall and the present Zhujiang New Town, has witnessed the development of Guangzhou city. In 2004, Tianhe District became the new city center of Guangzhou.

In 2010, the opening ceremony of Guangzhou Asian Games was held on a small island named Haixinsha in the Pearl River, and the Haixinsha Island is on the new axis of this city. It is said that the highest building, the largest public square, the largest underground space, the best cultural architecture and the most prosperous central business district locate here.

The Open Gene of Canton Fair

Guangzhou's stretching movement lies in not only the city's expansion, but also an open mind to the world. And it is the gene hidden inside the city's bone marrow and the city's unique spiritual temperament, which is mainly reflected in Canton Fair.

In 1957, the China Export Commodities Fair, an exhibition commonly called Canton Fair, was born in Guangzhou and opened a channel of communication between China and the world. The exhibition is "the No.1 exhibition in China" with the longest history, the highest level, the largest scale, the most complete types of goods, the largest number of buyers purchasing goods overseas and the best result of dealing.

Why should the first national exhibition of export commodities be held in Guangzhou? The reasons are unknown to outsiders. As a commercial city for thousands of years, Guangzhou has a strong commercial atmosphere, unique geographical advantages. It is the only channel for businessmen form Hong Kong, Macao and Southeast Asian to do business in the Chinese mainland.

In the early 1970s, Canton Fair was put into service in the new exhibition hall on Liuhua Road. Liuhua Pavilion is quite close to Guangzhou Railway Station, and keeps the Baiyun Airport within five or six kilometers' range of driving (but now it has moved from the city center to further suburbs, and it is called New Baiyun Airport to show the difference). In 1986, Liuhua Pavilion and its surrounding modern buildings such as Dongfang Hotel, Liuhua Hotel, the new Guangzhou Railway Station were named "Liuhua Yuyu", one of the eight attractions in Guangzhou.

Goat in the Chinese culture represents tameness. Because "goat" is pronounced the same with "sun" in Chinese, "goat" gets the meaning of auspiciousness. Because of a legend about goat, Guangzhou is also known as "Yangcheng". Since the beginning of Song Dynasty, people in the city has continually selected the eight attractions of the city, which called "Eight Attractions of Guangzhou".

In April 2001, in the eastern part of Pazhou which is more than 10 kilometers away from the Liuhua Pavilion, a new exhibition center was being constructed, and it was put into use in 2003. In October 2008, the 104th Canton Fair was held in Pazhou Complex.

Pazhou, the location of Huangpu Ancient Port, with Pazhou Convention and Exhibition Center, once again became a symbol of the communication between Guangzhou and the world.

With the arrival of the Internet era, Canton Fair also innovates constantly. It builds e-commerce platform to create an year-round online Canton Fair. Canton Fair embraces the Internet, so does Pazhou. Dozens of enterprises including Tencent, Alibaba, MIUI, Vipshop and so on gather in the agglomeration area of Internet innovations on the west side of Pazhou Island to set up headquarters or project companies.

WeChat is among them. The company WeChat belongs to is Tencent.

Pazhou Convention and Exhibition Center once again become a symbol of the communication between Guangzhou and the world.

Before the emergence of WeChat, their social software QQ was once the most popular one. Tencent purchased a piece of land in Pazhou at the price of 17.6 billion to build the headquarters building of WeChat, which is perhaps a way to show business ambitions.

It is believed that even after many years, Chinese people will remember in this era there is a social networking software called WeChat, which has a profound impact on their daily life. With "To connect everything" as its slogan, WeChat has become a software most Chinese people will install in their smart phones in this era. For a long time, it makes a lot of Chinese people do not need cash in their wallets, because online payment is so popular that you can pay directly by means of scanning QR codes even in a small shop in China's remote rural areas. The entire transaction process is done without cash.

In the second quarter of 2016, WeChat has already been installed in more than 94% of smart phones in China, and monthly active users have reached to 0.806 billion. Besides, its users cover more than 200 countries and speak more than 20 languages.

WeChat was born in Guangzhou. It connects China with the world in a special way, making the world more open.

WeChat and QQ are only Tencent's most representative products. Ma Huateng, the person in charge of this company, in the early stage of his business leads his own team to design webpages, to do system integration, and to do programming. But because of knowing nothing about marketing operation, they are often shut out when they promote their products to operators. Such experience, whether Bill Gates or Steve Jobs, should have been experienced.

In October 2016, the total number of China Mobile Net users in China has reached 1.077 billion, and the number of mobile Internet users is up to 1.02 billion, reaching a new record in its history, which is second to none in the world.

People bring the experience of the using Internet from the earlier desktop PC to all aspects of work and life. All areas can be always real-time online. With the use of WeChat, all industries are provided with a good foundation to develop online and offline businesses, which means a lot of opportunities. And the changes WeChat and its similar products bring to China are still on the way, far from ending.

Free Trade Zone: "the Welding Spot" Jointing the World

Draw a circle with Nansha as the center and 50 km as the radius circle. Such circle can include all major cities in the Pearl River Delta, including all ports and wharfs in Hong Kong and Macau. With a radius of 100 km the circle covers 9 cities in the Pearl River Delta and 5 major international airports. Geographically, Nansha is the center of the Pearl River Delta. But it is far from the economic development center. In China where it is believed that "Development is the absolute principle", Nansha seems to have verified the Chinese saying "black light" which means something locating at the center is intentionally or unintentionally ignored. In the 1980s, the wasteland Nansha, known as the "Siberia" in Guangzhou, is bleak and lifeless.

Huo Yingdong, an industrialist in Hong Kong, did not think so. Starting with lightering, and then engaging in real estate, he initiated the pattern of installment commonly used in the whole country. When he died in 2006, the official announcement was that he is "a close friend of the Chinese Communist Party", and in the eyes of Chinese people he is a trusted patriot. Like many Hong Kong people, Huo Yingdong's ancestral home is in Guangdong. He once built the Luoxi Bridge for his hometown Panyu in Guangzhou, so that the Pearl River no longer blocks the communication between two sides.

Huo Yingdong devoted huge sums of money and a lot of effort to Nansha. During his lifetime he repeatedly said that he had a "Nansha dream", and hoped to construct Nansha into an open window of Guangdong and even the whole country.

In 1992, Huo Yingdong bought 22 square kilometers of land in the coastal area of Nansha for operation and development. Since 2002, Nansha Hotel, World Trade Center and other landmarks as well as Dongfa Port, Nansha Coach Terminal, Humen Ferry Terminal, Nansha Information Technology Park had been constructed one after another. It is said that Huo Yingdong has invested 6 billion yuan within 25 years in Nansha. Such an amount of money is worth two Canton Tower (a shapely TV tower more than 400 meters), the landmark building of Guangzhou, or a tourist town covering an area of nearly 100 million square meters inland.

Solely relying on an enterprise, the speed of developing a vast land cannot be forcibly said to be fast, even though it cannot be said to be slow.

90% of the developed cities in the world locate in coastal areas. For example, in the United States, the most powerful country in the world, New York, Boston, Philadelphia, Washington, Seattle, San Francisco, Los Angeles, Houston, Atlanta, Miami are all coastal areas. The whole country of Japan is situated in a narrow coastal area. In the past, the development of Guangzhou has been dependent on the coastal areas of the Pearl River. Guangzhou is built near water and developed on water. However, with the development of the city, Guangzhou must move from relying on water to relying on the sea. As the only region nearing the sea in Guangzhou, Nansha undoubtedly becomes the core of its development.

Everything goes well! Nansha, together with Huo family, waits for a new opportunity. Now it seems that perhaps this opportunity should be called "Free Trade Zone".

In December 2014, the State Council decided to set up China (Guangdong) Pilot Free Trade Zone, Guangdong Free Trade Zone covers three areas: Nansha New Area in Guangzhou (Guangzhou Nansha Free Trade Zone), Qianhai and Shekou Area in Shenzhen (Shenzhen Free Trade Zone of Qianhai and Shekou), Hengqin New Area in Zhuhai (Zhuhai Hengqin Free Trade Zone), with a total area of 1162 square kilometers.

China Free Trade Zone is a new node for China to deepen reform and opening–up. Set up outside the customs and within the boundary of China, with tax preference and policies for special customs supervision as the main means and the trade liberalization and convenience as the main purpose, it is a multi–functional special economic zone. On September 29, 2013 China (Shanghai) Pilot Free Trade Zone was officially established, becoming the first free trade zone in China.

China (Guangdong) Pilot Free Trade Zone locates in three cities including Guangzhou, Shenzhen and Zhuhai. Guangzhou Nansha New Area covers an area of 60 square kilometers (including the area of 7.06 square kilometers of Guangzhou Nansha Bonded Port Area).

There is a detailed introduction to Nansha Pilot Free Trade Zone on the official website of Guangzhou Nansha New Area in China (Guangdong) Pilot Free Trade Zone: Nansha Pilot Free Trade Zone is committed to building a kind of legal international business environment in accordance with the new system of international rules, taking the lead in achieving service trade liberalization with Hong Kong and Macao, building an international shipping and logistics center with a high level of integration of international trade and financial innovation services, creating a demonstration base of the cooperation in technology and innovation between countries and regions along Maritime Silk Road, building a two-way channel and an important platform for Hong Kong and Macao to develop the mainland market and for the mainland via Hong Kong and Macao to develop international market, and playing an important role in building the new pattern of open economy.

Nansha Pilot Free Trade Zone is the first to implement the new model of "one counter handles all necessary formalities". It is the first in the country to expand the reform of "one business license one code" to 13 departments including industry and commerce, quality supervision, state tax and others, the first to provide the inspection service of government purchases, the first to implement the mechanism of customs quick inspection and release, and the first to create "wisdom inspection port".

Nansha Pilot Free Trade Zone created a remarkable "Speed of Free Trade Zone" in Guangdong.

Shenzhen: A "Young" City Keeps up with the World

The Great Changes of a Small Fishing Village

How long does it take for a small fishing village to develop into a large city? The answer Shenzhen gives is 30 years.

The Chinese take delight in sortation and ordering, such as the four major inventions and the five greatest warriors, and the city is the case. In the 1990s, people were used to abbreviating the three largest cities to "Jing–Jin–Hu" (Beijing, Tianjin and Shanghai). But in the beginning of this century, the three greatest cities referred to "Bei–Shang–Guang" (Beijing, Shanghai and Guangzhou). Around 2010, people were more accustomed to referring to the greatest cities as "Beijing, Shanghai, Guangzhou and Shenzhen". The up–and–coming youngster—Shenzhen has become a super city in China's city pattern and been widely accepted.

The supporters of special economic zones can say some successful examples, among them the most successful one is the one near Hong Kong and later known as the "Shenzhen miracle".

Because of the consideration of possible risks, China did not dare to implement economic reforms on a national scale. So, Shenzhen Special Economic Zone was established to do the test. Unexpectedly, it attracted thousands of foreign investors. The tested policy was immediately extended to other cities, including Shanghai subsequently.

Shenzhen has produced the first stock in China, auctioned the land market for the first time, created many new terms and lifestyles such as boss, going into business, stock company, migrant worker, fry cuttlefish and job–hopping. Over the past 30 years, Shenzhen has created innumerable "No. 1 in China".

The beginning of the reform in Shenzhen originates from the cry for

Luohu Port is located at the southern part of Luohu business center in Shenzhen. Separated from Hong Kong by a narrow river, Shenzhen is joined to Hong Kong through a two-decker foot bridge and a railway bridge. Luohu Port is one of the only two land ports in Shenzhen before reform and opening-up. Photographer: Da Guang

The Photo of Shenzhen shot from a high angle. Photographer: Wang Yubo

the construction of Shekou adjoining the bay. Yuan Geng is the most dazzling name in the history of Shenzhen Special Economic Zone and even the history of China's reform and opening–up. His keen determination on reform of and all kinds of exploration for Shekou industrial area seem to still have a significance on the present day.

China Merchants Bureau links the high–ranking offical in late Qing Dynasty Li Hongzhang in 1872 with the communist Yuan Geng in 1978.

In 1872, Li Hongzhang wrote a memorial to Tongzhi to request the establishment of the China Merchants, and the memorial was approved three days later. In October 1978, Yuan Geng, as the 29th head of the China Merchants Group, submitted *the Consultation on the Full Use of Hong Kong Merchants* to the Central Committee of the Communist Party of China, requesting the establishment of Shekou Industrial Zone, and the request was also approved three days later.

In 1978, Yuan Geng was 61 years old, the age called "a cycle of sixty years" in China. At this age, many people may have enjoyed their old age in peace, but Yuan Geng's new business has just begun.

He set up a board with words "Time is money, efficiency is life" on the road in Shekou, trying to break the life-long cadre employment system. And he published those articles which directly criticized him by pointing out his name in the newspaper. Faced with unwarranted accusations, Yuan Geng difficultly but also firmly carried out the reform in Shekou, from economic to political field, from social to cultural field.

Shekou's development and change is the epitome of Shenzhen's reform and opening-up.

From 1979 to 1988, during the ten years when he was in charge of the work in Shenzhen Special Economic Zone, the former Vice Premier of the State Council, Gu Mu, successively visited the Shenzhen Special Economic Zone for 12 times. Almost all major decisions in the early stage

Shenzhen Stock Exchange was opened on December 1st in 1990. Rooted in the frontier of China's reform and opening-up, serving China's economic development strategies, Shenzhen Stock Exchange is committed to build the most dynamic capital market platform in the world. Photographer: Da Guang

the special economic zone were formulated and implemented with his participation.

Wu Nansheng, who was responsible for the preparation of three special economic zones in Guangdong Province, first put forward "Guangdong takes the first step". And with the firm determination—"Kill me if you need to kill someone.", he took the initiative to apply for special economic zone.

Of course, the person most remembered with gratitude by people in Shenzhen is Deng Xiaoping. He named Shenzhen "Special Economic Zone", which occurred during the time from January 24 to February 5 in 1984, the time when Deng Xiaoping came to Guangdong to inspect Shenzhen.

Deng Xiaoping is the chief architect of China's economic and social reforms. In China, people are more willing to respectfully and courteously call him "Comrade Xiaoping".

In November 2000, a statue of Deng Xiaoping, was unveiled on the top of Lianhua Mountain in Shenzhen. It is the first statue of Deng Xiaoping approved by central government and erected in the form of urban sculpture in China.

The bronze statue of Deng Xiaoping on the top of Lianhua Mountain is 6 meters high and weighs 6 tons. The shaped Xiaoping is wearing a windbreaker, facing the south and striding forward, with a corner of the windbreaker flowing behind. When you climb from the north of Lianhua Mountain to the top of the mountain, the first thing come to your sight is the screen wall engraved with Deng Xiaoping's original words: "Shenzhen's development and experience have proved that our policy of establishing special economic zones is correct." The other side of the screen wall is write with clerical script, "I am a son of the Chinese people, and I deeply love my country and people in my country."

Located in Shenzhen, the giant portrait of Deng Xiaoping, has become one of the signs of Shenzhen. Many domestic and foreign tourists come here to cherish the memory of the old man who has changed China.

Around 1990, the international and domestic situation underwent profound changes. The development of the special economic zones, the reform and opening–up was again faced with obstacles. At such a critical moment, Deng Xiaoping once again came to Guangdong for inspection. It was during January 19 to January 29 in 1992 when he spent four days in Shenzhen and seven days in Zhuhai. On January 18 to February 21, Deng Xiaoping delivered important speeches in Wuchang, Shenzhen, Zhuhai, Shanghai and other places. He put forward the requirement of "taking advantage of good opportunities to speed up the pace of reform and opening–up, striving for a new level of national economy", which laid the ideological foundation for China to embark on the road of development of socialist market economy with Chinese characteristics.

On January 21, in China World Trade Center, Deng Xiaoping delivered the most important speech in the process of inspection. "China needs to be vigilant against the Right deviation, but primarily, it should guard against the 'Left' deviation. It has taken the special economic zones more than ten years to reach the present stage. They can collapse overnight! People will believe and support you only when the economy get developed and their lives become better. We must firmly adhere to the party's basic line of taking economic development as the central task not for ten years, twenty years but for a hundred years! The ways of not adhering to socialism, not reforming and opening–up, not developing the economy and not improving people's lives are all dead ends!"

The International Trade Building is known as the "the window of Shenzhen Special Economic Zone" and "a symbol of China's reform and opening up".

In 1984, the International Trade Building with a height of 160 meters and a total of 53 layers was completed after the construction was conducted for 14 months, creating a "three–days–a–floor" miracle. After the main building was started constructing, at the beginning it took 7 days to build a layer, then 5 days and then 4 days. From the 30th floor, the speed kept at three days one floor. The widespread "Shenzhen speed" as a result of the International Trade Building has become a new concept of high speed and high efficiency, and a symbol of China's construction and development after reforming and opening up.

The City of Immigrants

In just 30 years, Shenzhen has transformed from a small border town with a population of 3 million people and two or three narrow streets into a modern city with a population of 10 million people, prosperous economy, harmonious society, complete functions and beautiful environment, creating a miracle in the history of industrialization, urbanization and modernization of the world.

In Shenzhen's development process, there are more unknown people who make special contributions to the construction of this city. These contributions are seemingly insignificant but real, and become a great force to promote the city forward, which is in accordance with the Chinese ancient poem "Silent and soft, it moistens everything". This poem means that the spring rain quietly falls at night in the spring breeze, quietly moistening all things on the earth.

Shenzhen is the most typical immigrant city in China. In 1979, when Shenzhen was at the early stage of construction, the population was only thirty–odd million. By the end of 2015, the resident population has reached 113,789 million. Shenzhen has become a veritable city of immigrants and the largest immigrant city in China.

In July 1982, 20,000 infrastructure–construction engineering corps from Shanghai, Tianjin, Tangshan and other places assembled and went down south. They all transferred to construction workers, and a quarter of high buildings in Shenzhen in the 20th century was constructed by them.

In a sense, Shenzhen's history of 30 years is Shenzhen immigrants' history of struggling. They come here with dreams from all parts of the country. They grow out of nothing. They go through struggles, prosperity, confusion and transformation, enjoy the happiness of success and meet the new challenges together with the city.

The praise for these people in 2009 reached a special climax. In 2009, *Time* magazine in the United States selected Person of the Year, and Chinese workforce is one of them.

As the only group on the list, Chinese workforce ranks second only to the Federal Reserve Chairman. *Time* magazine has such a comment: "There is one word 'keeping 8%' in China. This word means maintaining an annual economic growth rate of 8%, which is essential to ensure social stability form the point view of the Chinese government. Many years ago, many people think this is a dream, but China has made it. As one of the major economic entities in the world, China continues maintaining the fastest pace of development, and leads the world to economic resurgence. These credits should first go to thousands of hard–working and persevering Chinese workers.

Whether in history or at present, Chinese workers are a great, outstanding and contributory team. Since the founding of new China, especially in the 30 years after reforming and opening–up, thousands of Chinese works have worked hard and made great contributions, paying an important role in promoting the economic development and social progress of China.

The night scene of Shenzhen. Photographer: Wang Yubo

The City of Innovation

In 2015, Huawei applied for 52,550 domestic patents and 30,613 foreign patents, with the total number of patent applications ranking first in the world. In 2015, Huawei, with the number of 3898, topped the list of patent rankings of global enterprises.

However, the number of applications does not mean the accumulation and advantages of a company on the aspect of patents. Only authorized patents can have real power! This is the reason why in 2015, Apple licensed 98 patents to Huawei in 2015, while Huawei licensed 769 patterns to Apple.

With the excellent quality, the newly born Huawei phones catch up with Apple and Samsung in the Chinese market.

Founded in 1987, Huawei Technologies Co. Ltd. is a private communications technology company which produces and sells communications equipment. At the end of 2016, he has more than 170,000 employees. Huawei's products and solutions have been applied in more than 170 countries around the world, serving for

45 operators out of the top 50 and 1/3 of the population of the world. In terms of the countries and population Huawei serves for, it is a global company with headquarters based in Shenzhen. It is a company developed from Shenzhen.

Huawei has become a symbol of innovation in Shenzhen and an exhibition displaying city's innovation and development. Shenzhen has been born for innovation, becoming the "City of Makers" and "City of Innovation" in the eyes of Chinese people. In addition to Huawei, there are some other famous companies in Shenzhen such as ZTE, Tencent, DJI and BGI.

Founded in 1998, Tencent, is one of the largest Internet integrated

Founded in 2006, DJI-Innovations (abbreviated as DJI), is the leading developer and producer of the control system and solutions of unmanned aerial vehicles. Photographer: Wang Yubo

service providers, but also one of the Internet companies with most service users in China. China's service users. The most well–known products of Tencent are QQ and WeChat. To some extent, these two products have already had their own implications, just like Chinese people will not only consider Apple to be a kind of fruits but also an American company and the products it produced.

The chairman of the board of Tencent, Ma Huateng, came to Shenzhen at the age of 13. In 1998, with 500,000 yuan of funds, he and his team of five people developed QQ software. Capital and technology have ever become the bottleneck of the development of Tencent, which made Ma Huateng sleepless all night. At the most difficult time, he wanted to sell QQ several times, but he insisted on keeping it. And the result turned out that in June 2015, the market value of Tencent ranked fifth in global Internet companies and the annual income of 2014 was 78.9 billion yuan.

The innovative and entrepreneurial DJI in field of advanced technology and BGI are considered examples of innovation in Shenzhen. DJI is known as the top–level company in the field of UAV with a global market share of more than 50%. Its products have been used for aerial photography, film, agriculture, news, energy, remote sensing mapping and many other areas, and continuing to integrate into new industries. BGI benefits human beings through the genetic science and technology. Founded in 1999, this company is the largest genomics research and development institution. It leads the development of genomics by means of the new developing pattern of "production–teaching–research" integration. Through the extensive cooperation between the branches around the world and the industry chain, BGI applies the frontier achievements in scientific research to medical health, agricultural breeding, resource preservation and other fields to promote the transformation of gene technology achievements, and further to benefit all people. BGI is selected into Global Growth Companies in 2015. General speaking, Global Growth Companies are regarded as market pioneers, innovators and builders.

It is not comprehensive to consider that the innovative ability of Shenzhen is represented by these well-known companies. "Independent innovation" has become the leading strategy for the development of the city. The research spending of Shenzhen is increasing year by year, with a proportion of 4.05% of GDP in 2015, which is twice the national average. PCT (Patent Cooperation Treaty) international patent applications and the invention patent ownership per ten thousand people of Shenzhen are at the first place among large and medium-sized cities in China. Besides, the innovation ability of Shenzhen finds a front position in the world in the

In 2015, the first "National Public Entrepreneurship and Innovation Week" of China was held. In 2016, the "National Public Entrepreneurship and Innovation Week" became big event of innovation industry. The picture shows the intelligent robot displayed on the "National Public Entrepreneurship and Innovation Week". Photographer: Wang Yubo

fields of 4G technology, gene sequencing, metamaterials and 3D display.

In 2014, Shenzhen PCT international patent applications reached 11600 with an increase of 15.9%, ranking first in large and medium–sized cities in China for 11 consecutive years. The invention patent ownership per ten thousand people reached 66.7, ranking first among major cities of China. In the list of ten Chinese innovators released by Forbes, Shenzhen accounted for 5 people. In 2014, two research results of Shenzhen were selected into the top ten scientific progress in China. Enterprises have become the major market players of Shenzhen and innovative actors.

As the most unique innovative city on the chain of global innovation, the youngest city in the first–tier cities in China, Shenzhen has been constantly exploring new economic growth impetus and developing the most suitable stage for global makers.

The Copycat Goes Away, the Wisdom Returns

After 30 years of reform and opening up, Shenzhen has had a relatively perfect downstream industry chain and formed a gathering area of science and technology, capital, information and talents in the field of hardware. When talking about his original intention of starting a business in Shenzhen, the founder of Seeed Studio, which is the largest open source hardware manufacturer in China, Pan Hao said that he was impressed by the prefect hardware in Shenzhen when he went around a whole day in Huaqiang North Commercial Area. Cyril Ebersweiler, the founder of the hardware incubation center HAXLR8R, an internationally renowned organization, moved its headquarters from Silicon Valley to Shenzhen. He said, "I can find any needed raw materials within 1 kilometer, which is impossible in the United States, Europe and even any other places in the world, because Huaqiang North Commercial Area can not be found in any other places." Another Indian businessman who settled in Shenzhen also said that any design, no matter how complex it is, can be produced in less

Shatoujiao is prosperous in business for its unique geographic location. Photographer: Da Gunag

than a week.

In Shenzhen, you can find any needed raw materials in the area less than 1 km away from Huaqiang North Commercial Area, and you can complete the whole process of "prototype–product–small batch production" within one week with only 1% to 5% of the cost in Silicon Valley. An entrepreneur who started a business in Zhongguancun asked his son: "Why must we go all the way to Shenzhen to start a business?" The son replied that it took only two weeks to find an IC in Shenzhen, but in other places the time spent may be two months. And there are many processing factories in Shenzhen and its surrounding areas. They produce good–quality and cheap PCB boards. This is an advantage of industrial chain that Shenzhen realized through the combination of the basic manufacturing industry and developed market economy. Such advantage makes the innovation in Shenzhen more convenient, making Shenzhen a "Paradise of Makers".

Huaqiang North Commercial Area ever received about 500,000 people per day on average and the its annual turnover was more than 300 billion yuan. It was the largest high–tech electronic products trading center with the most complete product categories and the largest annual turnover.

And it was once regarded as the "weather vane" and "barometer" of China's electronics industry. Here the turnover of electronic components accounted for 95% of the total number of electronic communications market in Shenzhen.

However, under huge turnovers, a variety of bogus electronic products are also emerging. After an Apple mobile phone comes into market, a month later you may spend several hundred yuan to buy a very similar phone with a new trademark of a bitten orange in Huaqiang North Commercial Area. With low price and fast updated speed, they shatter those domestic mobile phone brands which need both internal testing and network testing to pieces.

Therefore, Huaqiang North was once regarded as a pronoun of "shanzhai" and got into trouble by the name of the largest place producing fake mobile phones.

Copycat is usually called "shanzhai" in China. "Shanzhai" originally means the walled city in the mountain, and more often it refers to the product accused of imitation, copy and plagiarism.

If we say that copycat mobile phones can also make a profit, in the era of copycat tablet computers, a tablet computer at the price of about 200 yuan is everywhere. By selling copycat phones and tablet computers at low prices, copycat manufacturers quickly take roots and grow in Shenzhen, and then they are forced by low prices to shut down their companies and withdraw from the market.

Copycat and innovation are the two sides of a coin. Wang Jian, the chairman of the technical committee of Alibaba says in the book *Being Online*, "When most people ignore middle and small-sized enterprises like Huaqiang North, more people think these enterprises are fake, and we believe that they are promoting industrial changes."

Neil Goshenfield, the founder of Fab Lab believes that copycat is

China Hi-Tech Fair, the largest and most influential science and technology exhibition in present China, is held every year in Shenzhen and said to be the "First Science and Technology Exhibition in China". The fair has become an important window for the opening-up of China's hi-tech field. It plays an increasingly important role in promoting the commercialization, industrialization and internationalization of the achievements of high and new technology as well as promoting economic and technological exchanges and cooperation between countries and regions. Photographer: Wang Yubo

also a good way of innovation. He says that he likes Huaqiang North, and he has bought his son a product like AppleWatch which is better than AppleWatch and equipped with functions of mobile phones. It is also a kind of advanced technology to produce such a watch with many functions. In Fab2.0, we can also do some individuation manufacturing. Design, model and pack all functions to study how to copy this function instead of making a fake AppleWatch. "Here copy means that you have ability to go beyond the functional scope of the product."

At the end of 2010, Shenzhen began to organize crackdowns against intellectual property infringement and the production and sale of counterfeit and shoddy goods. After more than six months of crackdowns, more than 3600 merchants in Huaqiang North electronics market withdrew from the market, leading to a large-scale reshuffle of the mobile phone industry.

In addition, due to the construction of Shenzhen Metro Line 7, since March 2013, the main road in Huaqiang North was blocked for reconstruction. In Huaqiang North there once appeared the scene of

Huaqiang North Commercial Street.

vacant shops and declining rents.

At the end of 2016, Huaqiang North was opened again, making a stage pose as "pedestrian street" for the first time. Over the past 30 years, Huaqiang North has grown into "The First Street of China Electronics". In the next five to ten years, Huaqiang North will be committed to become "the most influential high-end electronic information service, display and trading center which radiates both home and abroad in China, a diversified and mixed high-quality commercial center, a manufacturing service center, and an integrated area with both business offices and living conditions".

Shenzhen has a clear understanding of innovation. Shenzhen intends to establish a comprehensive innovation ecosystem, and combine all kinds of innovative elements to form a positive oscillation through the innovation chain, that is, investing research funds earliest, and finally coming down through the results and financial innovations, and then returning to scientific research and innovation for a new round of innovation of higher technology and higher level. And a positive oscillation is thus formed.

Foshan：
A Blessed City

Chinese Cuisine Goes out of China

Shunde, together with Dongguan, Zhongshan and Nanhai, is called "Four Tigers in Guangdong" and at the first place of the top one hundred areas in China in 2014. In China's basic discourse system, the leading position in a list indicates the city's uniqueness.

Shunde, which means "following the way of Heaven and practicing morality", is a district of Foshan City, Guangdong Province. Since ancient times it has experienced developed economy, business prosperity as well as cultural and educational heyday.

Chencun rice noddle is a traditional dish of Chencun Town, Shunde District, Foshan City, Guangdong Province. Photographer: Lu Kaiyang

The roast suckling pig is glazed and cooked slowly over an open fire, and its skin is crisp and the fat is not greasy. With outstanding taste, Shunde Jun'an steamed pig and roast pig become the most well-known roast suckling pig. Photographer: Lu kaiyang

In December 2014, UNESCO awarded Shunde a plaque with words "Capital of Food"on it, so Shunde officially became a member of UNESCO Creative Cities Network.

At that time, there are six cities awarded the name of "Capital of Food" by the UNESCO in the world, namely, Popayan in Colombia, Chengdu in China, Ostersund in Sweden, Zahlah in Lebanon, Jeonju in South Korea and Shunde in Foshan, China.

Singh, director of the UNESCO office in Beijing, said, "Shunde, as a representative of Cantonese cuisine, has a very superior character and Shunde restaurants are around the world, which is very important for Shunde food to go abroad. In the future, we will also provide a more international platform to take Shunde food to the whole world."

Food has become one of the most important labels of Shunde, the city with an area of less than 1000 square kilometers. Chinese people show special preference for food culture, so there is an ancient proverb "Food is the first necessity of man.".

Cantonese cuisine is one of the Four Major Chinese Cuisines. Cantonese cuisine in the narrow sense refers to the Guangzhou cuisine, including Shun (de), Nan(hai) and Pan (yu).

Cantonese cuisine is famous in the world because of its strict selection of materials, fine workmanship, combination of Chinese and Western styles, delicious taste, health and other characteristics. As the most influential Chinese cuisine overseas, Cantonese restaurants are around the world, so there is a saying “Where there are ethnic Chinese there are Cantonese cuisine.”.

Shunde, one of the five districts of Foshan, is one of the most important birthplace of Cantonese cuisine. Shunde’s food culture is also a microcosm of Foshan. Roughly registered chefs and bakers are nearly a thousand in Foshan City, and many of them are national super–class master chef.

The statistics in 2014 show that Shunde, one of the places where there are most domestic chefs and noted restraurants, has 9 Chinese master chefs, 34 Chinese cooking teachers, 21 famous Chinese restaurants and 11 kinds of famous Chinese snacks. In 2004 it was chosen as “Hometown of Chinese Chefs” by the Chinese Cuisine Association. In 2010 it was named as “City of Chinese Food”. In Shunde, one of every 17 people may work in the restaurant industry.

For a century, many well–known chefs appear in the Foshan restaurant industry. Tao Taoju, Qimiaozhai and Datong restaurants, which were set up by Tan Jienan in the 1920s to 1930s, are still renowned in Guangzhou.

“Taotaoju” means delightedly drinking tea in the restaurant. Taotaoju, mainly engaged in tea–drinking and dining, is one of the most famous restaurants in Guangzhou. Cantonese people like drinking tea, especially drinking morning tea in restaurants. After guests sit down, the waiter come up and ask guests to order tea or pastries. Morning tea has become a unique urban culture in Guangzhou.

The famous chefs in the 1930s to 1950s, Cui Qiang, Li He, Wang Rui and Lu Zhen were known as the Four Heavenly Kings in Guangdong catering industry, and in the 1950s to 1960s there were Luo Kun and Pan Tong.

It is rare that the team of the two national chefs in Shunde, Xiao Liangchu and Kang Hui, successively set up state banquets in Beijing and Shanghai. From 1951 Xiao Liangchu as the chief chef worked in the national guesthouse in China, Shanghai Jinjiang Hotel, cooking and arranging dishes for the king, president, prime minister and prime minister from more than 100 countries.

In 1954 Premier Zhou Enlai attended the Geneva Conference, accompanied by Xiao Liangchu as a chef. Premier Zhou invited comedian Chaplin to dinner, and they talked delightedly. Chaplin finished eating and longed for more, so he specifically invited Xiao Liangchu to cook crisp fried chicken for packaging and sharing with families.

In 1961, Premier Chou Enlai led the Chinese delegation to attend the Geneva Enlarged Conference. Xiao Liangchu was asked to be the chef. His specialty Salt Baked Eight-Flavour Chicken was complimented by the guests from every contry.

Kang Hui was once the executive chef of the Beijing Hotel. He was responsible for the construction of the Diaoyutai State Guesthouse and the restaurant of the Great Hall of the People. In 2002, he was awarded one of the 12 Chinese master chefs in China.

Chinese Kung Fu Goes Abroad

Kung fu star Bruce Lee.

In 1999 *Time* magazine made a list of heroes and idols in the 20th century. On the list, there are the late British Princess Diana, the boxing champion Ali, Marilyn Monroe, US President Kennedy and Pele. But for Chinese, the most familiar one should be the yellow–skinned kung fu star Bruce Lee who often looks recalcitrant when he takes pictures. Like Michael Jordan is a sign of basketball and Bailey is a sign of modern football, Bruce Lee is the best endorser of Chinese Kung Fu.

In 2000, the US government

announced the release of a *Bruce Lee's 60th anniversary commemorative stamps*. Bruce Lee became the third artist after Marilyn Monroe and 007, and also the first Chinese who won this award. In 2003 the American magazine *Black Belt* launched the 30th anniversary of the death of Bruce Lee, indicating "Bruce Lee's long–term influence on American martial arts".

In English, Chinese martial arts are called kung fu, which is originally proverb of martial arts in the central region of Foshan and the Pearl River Delta. In language translation, the word–for–word transliteration may because it is difficult to translate or it is more important. Kung Fu clearly belongs to the latter. Undoubtedly it is Bruce Lee who make the world fall in love with Chinese Kung Fu.

Bruce Lee's ancestral home is in the town of Jun'an in Shunde, Guangdong, the hometown of kung fu. The largest Bruce Lee Memorial Hall in the world is in Jun'an. In 2008 the large exhibition hall with a total area of 370,000 square meters was shown to the public.

Foshan is the main source of southern Chinese martial arts. In 2004, Foshan was awarded the title of "City of Martial Arts". In the early Ming Dynasty, Foshan Kung Fu was quite popular. At the end of the Qing Dynasty and the beginning of the Republic of China, there were various schools of martial arts and appeared a group of martial arts masters and organizations with international influence. They went abroad and became globalized though various channels. Many kinds of Chinese boxing and schools such as the widespread Choy Lee Fut, Hong Boxing, Wing Chun are rooted in Foshan. The ancestral home of famous martial arts master Huang Feihong, Liang Zan, the master of Wing Chun, and Yip Man are also in Foshan.

Bruce Lee is well known to many people. He is a pioneer of the change of martial arts, martial arts attacker, martial arts philosopher, the

The Wing Chun master Yip Man who learned and became a master in Foshan is renowned at home and abroad.

founder of UFC, the father of MMA father, martial arts master, founder of martial arts films, founder of Jeet Kune Do, Chinese film actor of martial arts, the first global promoter of Chinese martial arts and the first Chinese Hollywood actor. His four and a half films in Hong Kong broke many records for three times. Among them, the film *Way of the Dragon* broke the record of Asian film box office. The global total box office of the film *Way of the Dragon* shot through the cooperation with Hollywood reached 2.3 billion US dollars. The American newspaper even described Bruce Lee as "Kung Fu King", and the Japanese called him "Warrior Saint", while Hong Kong newspapers praised him as "Wizard of modern Chinese Kung Fu and in the film history".

It is after Bruce Lee when many Chinese stars of martial arts step on the world stage. Jackie Chan and Jet Li are among them.

Different from Bruce Lee, who directly shows the firmness of Kung Fu, Jackie Chan connects martial arts with opera juggling, which reduces bloody violence scenes commonly seen in martial arts films while paying attention to the viewing quality of actions, and opens a new space of Kung Fu comedies.

Looking back to the past, Bruce Lee was born in the United States, but his childhood and youth was spent in Hong Kong. The little Bruce Lee was very thin and weak. In order to build up his body, his father taught him to play tai chi. Bruce Lee himself was fond of trying new things and adventure, especially outdoor sports. So, he completely fell in love with martial arts. In addition to tai chi, he also learned Wing Chun, Hong Boxing and Shaolin Boxing, laying foundation for the future creation.

In 1967, at the age of 27, Bruce Lee founded the world–wide modern Chinese Kung Fu Jeet Kune Do which is without the limitation of schools in the United States. This is a kind of all–round free sparring combining the essence of various martial arts in the world. But many people think that Jeet Kune Do resembles Wing Chun to some extent. There is no doubt that such resemblance comes from his teacher Yip Man.

The ancestral home of Yip Man, born in 1893, is in Sang Yuan in

Yewen Hall collects and exhibits materials about how Yip Man carries forward Wing Chun.

Nanhai County, Guangdong. In the 1950s, he began to teach Wing Chun in Hong Kong. His disciples, Liang Ting, carried forward Wing Chun to the world, forming a set of the most authoritative traditional Chinese martial arts practice course *WingTsun* that is famous in the world. After Yip Man passed away in 1972, his two sons Ip Chun and Ip Ching were committed to promoting Wing Chun internationally. Ip Chun also won awards issued by US Olympic Committee.

Another Chinese Kung Fu star Jet Li was born in Beijing. He set a record for consecutively winning the all–round champion of Chinese martial arts in 1975 to 1979. Had not he starred in the film *Shaolin Temple* in 1982, he might be just a good martial arts player rather than a martial arts star.

The sensation caused by *Shaolin Temple* can be seen from the fact that the mainland the total domestic box office was up 100 million yuan with the ticket purchased at the price of 0.1 yuan. In other words, his film was watched at least 1 billion times.

The most classic movies shot starred by Jet Li are the series of *Once Upon a Time in China*. At the beginning of 90, Jet Li accepted the invitation of starring in *Once Upon a Time in China*, causing a sensation in Hong Kong, after which he starred in series of five *Once Upon a Time in China* films. In China, the movies shot on the theme of Fei–hung Wong are up to hundreds, creating a record in the world.

Of course, the character Fei–hung Wong in these films is not the same with the reality. Fei–hung Wong was born in Nanhai County, Foshan City in 1856. He is a master of Hong Boxing at the end of the Qing Dynasty and the beginning of the Republic of China and a grandmaster in the field of martial arts in Lingnan. He has an important influence on the development of southern Chinese martial arts. Fei–hung Wong is a legendary figure. He ever followed the famous patriotic generals Liu

Yongfu in the anti–Japanese war to defend Taiwan. Also, he is a noted life–saving doctor with a big heart. What's more, he is good at lion dance and called Guangzhou lion king.

Dreams of Foshan

Food and martial arts make Foshan well-known in the world and become a cultural city and the core area of Cantonese culture. Equally important, Foshan is known as the national advanced manufacturing base and an important manufacturing center in Guangdong.

Foshan was started in Jin Dynasty and got the name in Tang Dynasty. 500 years ago, in the late Ming Dynasty in the traditional agricultural country, the division of labor in manufacturing process was more refined, and the class of handicraftsmen who broke away from agricultural cultivation appeared. At that time, the commodity economy was seeded in China, especially in the four places known as the "Four Famous Towns in Ancient China", namely, Hankow Town in Hubei, Jingdezhen in Jiangxi, Zhuxian Town in Henan and the known-to-us Foshan Town in Guangdong.

The city we are going to talk about is Foshan, a town that stepped onto the stage of Chinese history 500 years ago. It is

Overlooking Foshan. Photographer: Li Xihua

during this period that Foshan rapidly developed into an economic, business and cultural center in Southern China.

During the Ming and Qing Dynasties, Foshan gradually developed into a goods distribution centers in Lingnan—to the area south of the Five Ridges, the manufacturing center of metallurgical casting, ceramics, textile, Chinese patent medicines.

Shiwan is located at the southeast of Chancheng District in Foshan, where, with the saying that "Shiwan tiles well-known overseas are the best in the world". The ceramic here has long been a bright "business card" of Foshan. In the Ming and Qing Dynasties, there are 107 ceramics with more than 60,000 people working in the nearby area for several

Shiwan ceramics enjoy high reputation. The picture shows visitors watching the exhibition in Foshan. Photographer: Li Xihua

kilometers around Shiwan Town. Because of Shiwan ceramics, Foshan is named "Pottery Capital in the South". "Du" in Chinese has a meaning of "leader" which means the best. After the reform and opening up, Shiwan ceramics are much more widely distributed, more diverse in kinds and larger in scales.

Even more incredibly, as a center of four kinds of manufacturing industries, Foshan does not produce drug, cotton, iron mine and clay. Such phenomenon is vividly described as "creating something out of nothing".

As a matter of fact, the flourishment of the handicraft industry in

Foshan has something to do with the southward migration of outcomers. In the late period of Southern Song Dynasty, in order to avoid wars, Chung Yuan population along with handicraftsmen moved to the South. In the Ming and Qing Dynasties, the development of handicraft industry in Foshan came to its peak. Handicraft industry spread all over more than 620 streets and 60 ferries, forming twenty–eight special commercial shops of all walks of life.

In 1872, the 36–year–old Chen Qiyuan from Jian Village in Xiqiao Twon, Nanhai, Guangdong came back home from Southeast Asia. In the next year, by using self–designed machines, he founded the first national capital enterprise of silk reeling industry. At the age of 25, he went to Vietnam with his brother to do business. Perhaps in order to express the good expectation of "maintaining flourishment", he gave the factory the name of "Jichanglong".

Jichanglong Silk–Filature Factory was large in scale. Owing to good management, the business of the factory flourished, and its products were sold at home and abroad, bringing in a large amount of income. For the benefit of his hometown, he built luxurious "Baiye Lane" living buildings in Jian Village, which made him become a world–famous rich businessman.

Jichanglong Silk–Filature Factory is the first mechanized silk–filature factory run by national capital in China. Its establishment marked the beginning of a new historical period of the reeling industry, and promoted the development of the reeling industry in the Pearl River Delta and even the whole country.

Foshan also gave birth to first matches factory, Qiaomin Matches Factory, in China. In 1879 the young Wei Shengxuan, the founder of the factory, witnessed that the input of matches from abroad brought about the outflow of domestic wealth. Hence, he went to Japan to learn matches manufacturing techniques. After coming back home, he founded Qiaomin Matches Factory in Wenchangsha District in Foshan.

Symbolized by the first new–style silk–filature factory and matches factory in China, Foshan which leads new trends has become one of the birthplaces of modern national industry.

Today, Foshan has become one of the most important business centers in the Pearl River Delta Economic Zone, a national model city of logistics with a batch of logistics trading, a distribution center with large–scale investment and strong radiation capability. Foshan is one of the six China capital of brands, the exemplary city of the implementation of national trademark strategies and a city of brand economy in China. As a major manufacturing city, Foshan has a long history of industrial development, especially the traditional manufacturing industry, including Midea, Haitian and many other well–known enterprises with touring elements. Represented by Shiwan ceramics, the ceramic manufacturing industry owns hundreds of various types of industrial tiles and sanitary products. Represented by the watered gauze, illuminations and jade, the old–line art industry has become a perfect representative of humanity history. Represented by the Haitian soybean sauce and Shunde sugar, the food industry has witnessed the development process of food industry in Lingnan.

Dongguan: The Manufacturing City Facing Difficulties

The Miracle between Two Cities

Dongguan is located on the east coast of the Pearl River estuary. The Pearl River, the third largest river in China, flows into the sea via Guangdong, nourishing a few of cities, including Dongguan. These cities are known as the Pearl River Delta, which is one of most economically developed areas in China. In particular, Dongguan locates between the two major cities of Guangzhou and Shenzhen, within one–hour drive from the central urban area of Guangzhou and Shenzhen, but miraculously created a completely different way of growth form the two cities, keeping its own spirit.

One foreign expert once said, "More than 10 years ago, from the point of view of the satellite map, the area between Guangzhou and Shenzhen was blank. Within a few years, a city appeared in this blank." This is undoubtedly a miracle in the urban–construction and economic history of China.

Dongguan, whose fast development astonishes people, is the epitome of the development of Chinese cities and even

Dongguan is the historical and cultural city in Guangdong.

China. Guancheng is a town in Dongguan. A town in China is a unit of administrative division at the level or below the level of county. Usually below a prefecture–level city is a county below which is a town. However, Dongguan has become a "special one". It is one of the few prefecture–level cities below which there are no districts and counties, commonly known as "Zhitongzi City".

Guancheng is only one of more than 30 streets and towns in Dongguan, but it has always been the political, economic and cultural center of Dongguan City, with a long history and profound cultural heritage.

In China, cultural heritage is mainly reflected in the history of a city. Keyuan Garden, one of the four famous gardens in Qing Dynasty in Guangdong, a major historical and cultural site protected at the national level, is seated in the thousand–year–old ancient city. "Keyuan" means "can be visited and appreciated". Keyuan Garden was a gathering place for literati at that time. As a major historical and cultural site protected at the national level, Keyuan Garden takes an important place in the modern art and architectural history of Guangdong.

Chinese people are used to talking about Tang Poetry and Song Ci. Su Shi has received high attainments in the aspects of articles, poems and ci (a type of classical Chinese poetry in Song Dynasty). He can be called as the representative of the highest literary achievements of Song Dynasty. There is an unbeknown story between him and the Zifu Temple in Dongguan. He not only slept over in Zifu Temple, but also wrote three articles in 1100: *Memory in Arhat Pavilion in Zifu Temple in Dongguan County of Guangzhou*, *Inscription on the Stupa in Zifu Temple in Dongguan County of Guangzhou*, and *Praise for the Rebirth of the Cypress in Zifu Temple in Dongguan County on Guangzhou*, which are passed down to now.

Guangdong Guanyinshan National Forest Park in Zhangmutou Town, Dongguan City

Searching “Guancheng” in Baidu, you will first see the webpage titled “Cultural Guancheng”, from which the unique status of culture in the city and traces left by the city can be seen. In fact, this is the official website of Wancheng Street Office. Baidu, most well–known in the field of network–searching, can be simply understood as google of China. Its name is said to be derived from a well–known Chinese poem, “Time and time again, I searched for you in the crowd. Suddenly, I spun around and saw the very you standing amidst thin lights.” This poem is the representative works of a famous Ci writer in Song Dynasty. Isn’t “searching for her time and time again” a true portrayal of network search.

The webpage introduces Guancheng like this: Guancheng Streets in Dongguan City have a long history of 1700 years. Since A.D. 757, it has been the location of the government of Dongguan city. It has a long history of culture and a lot of cultural relics.

Not Just "Destroying Opium at Humen Beach"

Dongguan is known to Chinese people partly because of "Destroying Opium at Humen Beach". In the 1880s, due to the sharp increase in opium input, the trade status of China and Britain changed completely, with Britain changing from import surplus into the export surplus and China changing from export surplus to import surplus, which resulted in quantities of silver outflow. According to statistics, between 1820 and 1840, China's outflow of silver was around 100 million. The constant outflow of silver caused by the large number of opium imports has begun to disrupt the national treasury and currency circulation of Qing Dynasty, which put Qing's economy on the brink of collapse. More seriously, the spread of opium greatly devastates the physical and mental health of the smokers, and no country can tolerate its development. In June 1839, Qing government appointed the imperial envoy Lin Zexu to destroy opium on Humen beach in Guangdong. With the 23 days from June 3 to 25, 19187 boxes and 2119 bags of opium with a total weight of more than 100 million kilograms were destroyed. Humen, the town near sea in Dongguan, became famous at home and abroad because it turned the page of the modern history of China.

The Ban-smoking Sculpture. Photogr--apher: Da Guang

Lin Zexu spent his whole life in fighting against the invasion of foreign enemies. Because of his advocacy of prohibition of opium, in China, he is regarded as a "national hero". But he is open to Western culture, technology and trade, advocating learning and using their strengths. Based on documents, he has at least a slight acquaintance with English and Portuguese and puts efforts to translate Western newspapers, magazines and books. Wei Yuan, a thinker in late Qing Dynasty, complied the documents translated by Lin Zexu and his assistants as *Illustrated Annals of Overseas Countries* from which the Westernization Movement in late Qing Dynasty and even Japan's Meiji Restoration has drawn inspirations.

The event of "Destroying Opium at Humen Beach" makes Dongguan a place where many people have not been to but heard of. However, it is impossible for a city to be respected for only some moments in history. "Dongguan miracles" created since the reform and opening up are known as "a wonderful and vivid miniature of China's reform and opening up", become an advanced model of China's reform and opening up, which is a

The Ban-smoking Sculpture on Humen Taiping Square.

more important reason of our continuing concentration on this city.

The Third Plenary Session of the Eleventh Central Committee (its full name is the third plenary session of the Eleventh Central Committee of the Communist Party of China) was held. In *How China Became Capitalist*, Ronald Harry Coase, the winner of the Nobel Prize in Economics and the originator of the new institutional economics, on the road to China's market economy, commented on the conference like this, "a decisive event in the history of the People's Republic; it re–consolidated the power of the Party and paved the way for the reunification of a fractured society. The decisions made there would re–channel the energy, enthusiasm, and creativity of the Chinese people from the politics of class conflict to socialist modernization."

Around this conference, China has gradually implemented a policy of reform and opening up.

In November 1978, Xiaogang Village in Fengyang County, Anhui Province, began to implement the household contract responsibility system of "parceling out lands to individual households, responsible for one's own profits and losses", which opened the curtain of China's internal reform.

In July 1979, Guangdong province and Fujian province were formally approved to carry out special policies and flexible measures in foreign economic activities, and took a historical step of reform and opening up.

Before the reform and opening–up, in Dongguan, the lowest income of a labor is only a few cents. But 30 years later, in 2008, the average annual growth rate of Dongguan economy increased by 18%, creating a high–growth miracle with a faster speed and longer cycle than the early development of "Four Asian Tigers". Dongguan has become one of the fastest growing economies in China. And in terms of comprehensive economic status, it has been on the twelfth position among big and medium–sized cities in China. In fact, the area of Dongguan is not larger or even smaller than many counties in the mainland.

"Asian Four Dragons" in the English world is called "Four Asian Tigers". Dragon is one of the most representative cultural symbols of the Chinese nation. The "Four Asian Tigers" refers to that from the 1960s, Hong Kong, Singapore, South Korea and China Taiwan have implemented the export–oriented strategy focusing on the development of labor–intensive processing industry. Within a short time, Dongguan has achieved the economic take–off, become a developed and rich area in Asia, and been regarded as the representative of the rise of Asian economy. For a long time, the "Four Asian Tigers" became a good example of China, especially the coastal provinces.

On his inspection tour in the south in 1992, Deng Xiaoping put forward that Guangdong should strive to catch up with the "Asian Four Tigers" in 20 years. Dongguan is located in Guangdong province whose economic aggregate has long been 1/7 of the economic aggregate of China. By reference to the national economy in the world, Guangdong is equal to South Korea, ranking twelfth in the world.

Through the development of Guangdong, we can see the development process of Dongguan. Callas, the former chief Asia–Pacific economist of the World Bank, has been quite amazed at "Dongguan miracle": "Dongguan, known as 'world factory', a city in southern China, which in the past 20 years has maintained an annual growth rate of 20%, within its territory 95% of the needed components for manufacturing and assembling computers are accessible."

Callas also said in his academic report "An East Asian Renaissance: Ideas for Economic Growth" that in 1978, Dongguan was a collection of villages and small towns. The area's population relied primarily on fishing and farming. the Pearl River is only a large town in 1978, its population mainly by fishing and farming for a living. Dongguan today has a population of nearly 7 million. More than 5 million of the inhabitants are migrants who work in the thousands of factories that dot the city, creating a dizzying range of products.

Dongguan Model

What is the secret of Dongguan? Or what is the secret of China's rapid economic development? One and maybe the most important answer is to make use of foreign capital and take the path of developing export-oriented economy.

In July 1978, the State Council (the Central People's Government, the executive organ of the supreme organ of state power in China and the highest administrative organ of the state) issued the *Trial Measures for Carrying out Foreign Processing and Assembling Operations*. Guangdong, as the leading area and frontier of China's reform and opening up, is the first to make decision of processing materials supplied by clients. By utilizing its own geographical advantages and the advantageous relationship with numerous overseas Chinese, Hong Kong and Macao compatriots, Dongguan began to introduce foreign investment. Due to the shortage of capital, technology and talent, "the three-processing and one compensation" is taken as the starting point of processing trade.

"The three–processing and one compensation" refers to materials processing, sample processing, assembling with provided parts and compensation trade, which is a form of trade tentatively created at the beginning of the reform and opening–up in China. In the framework of "the three–processing and one compensation", the main structure of a company is as follows: foreign clients provide equipment (building factories with foreign investment), raw materials, samples, and are responsible for the export of all products; Chinese enterprises are responsible for providing land, plant and labor. Through the cooperation between Chinese and foreign parties, a new enterprise of "The three–processing and one compensation" is founded.

The first "the three–processing and one compensation" enterprise in the mainland of China, Taiping Handbag Factory was born in Dongguan. This factory, whose predecessor is a Taiping Bamboo Ware House, was set up on September 15, 1978 in Guangdong with an industrial and commercial approval number of YUZI001.

In July 1978, Hong Kong Xinfu Handbag Company with nearly three hundred staff was due to pushed to the brink of collapse due to continuing rising costs. The boss Zhang Zimi came to Humen in Dongguan with a few handbags and some pieces of cloth and found a young man named

The Taiping Handbag Factory with historical meaning.

Tang Zhiping.

The 26–year–old Tang Zhiping was responsible for the supply and marketing business in Taiping Garment Factory. Zhang Zimi took out of a black ladies' handbag and some cut–parts of semi–finished handbags, hoping that the Taiping garment factory could produce such a handbag by imitation as soon as possible.

Once a Chinese media reported such a scene: (Zhang Zimi) took out of a black artificial leather handbag from his bag and asked workers to reproduce a same handbag without any drawings and instructions, which is a problem they had never touched upon. So, three workers who had never seen such a handbag stayed up the whole night to produce a similar handbag with a little raw leather provided by Hong Kong customers and sewing machines. Guests were very satisfied, and a month later they signed a five–year contract with the Second Light Industry Bureau of Guangdong (Taiping Garment Factory was an enterprise below the Second Light Industry Bureau of Guangdong). The first enterprise of "the three–processing and one compensation" was officially unveiled in Dongguan.

Taiping Handbag Factory is located at No. 7 on Jiefang Road in Humen Town, a place where the event of "Destroying Opium at Humen Beach" once took place and again created another No.1 of China. The honorable "YUZI001" went out of business in 1996. However, because of its irreplaceable historical labels, it is often mentioned by Chinse people including the people of Dongguan.

In Dongguan, it became a trend to make use of foreign capital. Enterprises of "the three–processing and one compensation" in Dongguan sprang up like mushrooms.

By the end of 1988, in Dongguan there were more than 2500 enterprises of "the three–processing and one compensation" spreading over 80% of the villages. In 1991, the foreign investment was up to 1.7

billion US dollars. Dongguan has developed from an unknown small agricultural town into a well−known industrial city.

The success of enterprises of "the three−processing and one compensation" has aroused nationwide concern. Such development pattern had also been widely adopted throughout the country. And it has become a nationwide trend to absorb foreign investment to develop economy. A lot of people from coastal areas came to Dongguan to study and learn from Dongguan's successful practice. Some media and economists also stopped in Dongguan and summed up the successful practice into the "Dongguan model" which enjoys a good reputation in China.

The statement that "It doesn't matter whether the cat is black or white, as long as it catches mice." is praised as a theory of the chief designer of China's reform and opening up. This theory expresses a view of proceeding from actual conditions all the time, rather than from rules and regulations. The construction of socialism is realized by actual doing on the consideration of developing social economy, enchaning national comprehensive power and improving people's living standards, instead of talking. This theory has undoubtedly advocated a spirit of working in earnest. The similar widespread statement is "To cross the river by feeling the stones", which also emphasizes the importance of gaining experience from practice. It is precisely because of this, based on practical situations, different places explore different ways of development, and the exploration is summarized as a model.

"Dongguan model" was once the basic model of the implementation of coastal development strategies in China. It is as famous as "Southern Jiangsu model" and "Wenzhou model", each representing different types of economic development model. Coincidentally, these three models take place in the provinces with strong economic strength in China, "Southern Jiangsu model" in Jiangsu Province, "Wenzhou model" in Zhejiang

Province.

"Southern Jiangsu model" refers to the way adopted by Jiangsu, Wuxi and Changzhou in southern Jiangsu province to achieve non–agricultural development by developing township enterprises. The main features of the model are as follows: farmers rely on their own strength to develop township enterprises; the pattern of ownership of township enterprises gives priority to collective economy; the township government dominates the development of township enterprises; market regulation is the main means.

Wenzhou people are called Chinese Jews. In the whole country, they are part of those who are most sensitive to the market. They can always capture market opportunities and find the market demand at the earliest. Under the nurture of the market, Wenzhou people spare no effort to develop light manufacturing industry. All of a sudden family workshops are all over the city. Wenzhou people's small commodities quickly become famous all over the world. The "Wenzhou Model" based on small commodities refers to that, Wenzhou, the southern part of Zhejiang province, develops non–agricultural industries through the cottage industry and professionalized market, as a result of which, the development pattern of small commodities and big market is formed. Small commodities refer to the commodities with small production scale, low technical content and transportation costs. Large market refers to the market network established by Wenzhou people in the whole country.

New development needs even make new demands on government management services. To meet the need of reform and opening up and attracting foreign businesses and investment, Guangdong takes the lead in setting up the country's first processing trade services office, providing one package service for people who start business in Dongguan with all departments working together to solve problems for enterprises and people, which has greatly accelerated the speed of the introduction of foreign investment into Dongguan.

In 2007, with only 0.03% of the national land area, Dongguan created 1.3% of GDP, 1.1% of the fiscal revenue and 4.9% of the total exports, going beyond the economic energy of some provinces in the mainland. So, the outside world uses "richer than a province" to describe the economic capacity of Dongguan.

It is in the process of economic development, Dongguan rapidly while quietly conducts urbanization and develops from an agricultural county to an industrial big city. Around 1990, the booming scene of "village fire, household smoke" could be seen everywhere in the rural areas of Dongguan. Some people summarized such urbanization as "rural urbanization of urban–rural integration".

China's urbanization rate reached 57.35% in 2016. Figures show that by 2020, China's urbanization rate will reach 60%. In 1978, this figure was only 17.9%. Urbanization is the process of human progress must go through, through the urbanization, marking the realization of the goal of modernization.

In 1984, the reform and development of the rural areas in China was still in the stage of perfecting the household contract responsibility system. However, Dongguan had already completed rural economic management system and started to change to the commodity agriculture. Due to the rapid development of the township enterprises, the labor force was accelerated to change to the non–agricultural industry. So, in that year, Dongguan put forward the goal of "marching into rural industrialization".

Rural industrialization has promoted the process of urban–rural integration and urbanization. In 1992, Dongguan established the strategy of "building Dongguan in accordance with the modern urban structure", which soon makes Dongguan from the original rural town into the group city with characteristics of urban–rural integration. Since 2001, Dongguan has set off a new upsurge of urban construction.

Like many developing cities in China, the visual boundaries of the city and the countryside are no longer so clear, and in countryside too many western–style buildings have been built. In recent years, it has been popular for urban people to travel and live in rural areas. However, 30 years ago, it is the very countryside where they want to leave.

Benefiting from the rapid economic development, Dongguan took the lead in the implementation of agricultural tax exemption, popularizing high school education, exempting urban and rural students from tuition and incidental fees as well as textbooks fees at the stage of compulsory education in Guangdong. Dongguan also took the lead in implementing the farmer (town dweller) endowment insurance, the farmer (town dweller) basic medical insurance as well as endowment insurance designed for family planning.

Some people think that this path represents the direction of the urbanization and modernization of Chinese rural areas. The research office of the General Office of the CPC Central Committee once pointed out: "Dongguan Road has provided a realistic and feasible model of urbanization in China", and will "provide some important inspirations for China's modernization".

"The Traffic Jam in Dongguan, the Stockout in the World"

Things are constantly changing, some in the right direction.

Despite of the amazing development achievements achieved in the 1980s, Dongguan does not lie on its laurels and constantly looks for new opportunities. At that time, Dongguan basically developed labor−intensive industries with low technical content and low added value, mainly relied on the increase in foreign labor to support economic growth, which is an extensive method of economic growth.

With the entry of more and more IT companies and the formation of IT communities, Dongguan's economy has undergone profound changes. The total exports of Dongguan increased from US $39 million in 1978 to US $ 60.232 billion in 2007, with an increase of 1543.4 times and an average annual growth rate of 27.7%. Dongguan became the city with the third highest export volume after Shenzhen and Shanghai, and ranked first among prefecture−level cities.

There are two sayings, that is, "If Dongguan is in traffic

jam, the world will be out of stock." and "If Dongguan is in traffic jam, the world will have a cold.". Because here the production of computer motherboards, magnetic heads and drives accounts for more than 75% of the total production in the world. "No matter where you place orders, the place of production is Dongguan." It is a fact that Dongguan has become a modern manufacturing city.

Dongguan needs to and must achieve the transformation and upgrading of industrial structure and transform into a more advanced mode of economic development. In 1994, Dongguan announced that Dongguan had basically achieved the industrialization of the countryside, which is the end of Dongguan's "First Industrial Revolution", and the next step is

Dongguan Songshan Lake High-tech Development Zone has become the banner of independent innovation in Dongguan.

to seize the opportunity in good time to promote the "Second Industrial Revolution."

"Second Industrial Revolution" refers to the rapid transformation of labor–intensive industries into technology–intensive industries and the slow transformation of "quantitative" economy into "quality" economy, whose proposal and implementation marks the beginning of upgrade and transformation of Dongguan economy.

Dongguan has seized rare opportunities and undertaken the second wave of international industry transfer. At that time, the advanced IT industry developed rapidly in Dongguan. Known as the "IT capital in China", Dongguan held the E–business Expo which became one of the four major international computer information Expos. Dongguan is the largest computer components manufacturing base in the world. 95% of the computer components are produced in Dongguan.

Within more than 30 years, starting from the way of "the three–processing and one compensation", the industrial level of the export–oriented economy of Dongguan is continually rising and the product connotation is continually upgrading. Into the 1980s, Dongguan mainly undertook traditional manufacturing industry with small business scale and low additional value, such as Hong Kong textile, shoemaking, bag and luggage making and toymaking. Into the 1990s, the IT manufacturing industry based on computer peripheral products from Taiwan, Japan and South Korea flooded into Dongguan, so Dongguan became a manufacturing capital.

Of course, IT mannfactuning industry is far from enough. Dongguan finally formed a manufacturing system with complete range, perfect facilities and advanced technology, covering more than 30 industries and more than 60,000 kinds of products. Most industrial products in the world can find their supporting industry and products in the "industrial biologic chain" of Dongguan enterprise groups. In a sense, Dongguan is the sample region of "MADE IN CHINA". In Dongguan, you can always find a sample to analyze any sign of disturbance or trouble about the manufacturing industry. Dongguan has become a "foundry" for various types of manufacturing of electronic information, electrical machinery and equipment, textile, footwear and headwear, food and beverage, paper and paper products.

Dongguan is also a capital of shoes, clothing and toys. One of every ten pairs of shoes in the world are manufactured in Dongguan. It is still a "Capital of Garments". In Dalang Town in Guangdong, a place where there are almost no seasonal changes, someone can still wear short−sleeved T−shirts in December and a place does not produce any wool. Annually it sells more than 10 billion pieces of sweater, which means that in every five people in the world there is a man who wear a sweater produced in Dalang Town.

Jiangmen:
Still a Door to Sea

The "Hometown of Overseas Chinese" with Outstanding People and Smart Land

After we finished dinner at Chen's little school, the heat of the day had already diminished. The sun retreated behind the hills, leaving brightly colored clouds hanging in the sky, over the hills and trees.

We walked through a gravel path, and before long we reached the bank, where a pavilion stood made of straw. Filing through the pavilion, we found several small boats anchored under two big trees along the bank.

One after another, we hopped into one of the boats. One friend loosened the rope, pushed the bamboo pole against the bank, which moved the boat to the center of the river.

The river was wide, the water glistening without a ripple. The boat was steadily floating on the water, the three oars pulling in rhythm.

Then the river narrowed at a certain point. Clusters of leaves stretched out touching the water's surface. The leaves were in a lovely green color. There seemed to be many lush banyan trees, but I couldn't make out where the main trunks of the trees were.

My friends immediately corrected me as I referred to them as being many banyan trees. One of them said it was only one banyan, and another said there were two. I had seen many enormous banyans before, but it was the first time I saw such a gigantic one.

As the boat drew nearer to the banyan, I finally got a good look at it. This was a huge tree, with countless branches, on which grew aerial prop roots. Many of the roots were dangling to the ground, some all the way into the soil. There were branches hanging above the water. Seen from a distance, the tree seemed to be reposed on the water.

It was in the lush season. The banyan seemed to showcase its vibrant life energy to us. There were many leaves, clusters over clusters, with not even a tiny hole existing. The emerald green shining brightly in front of our eyes, it was like on each leaf there was a new life dancing. What a tree it is growing in the beautiful southern part of China!

The boat was moored under the tree for a moment, but we didn't get onto the bank because it was so wet. A friend said it was known as the "paradise of the birds" here. The local peasants forbade anyone to catch these birds. I thought I had heard some sounds of flapping wings, but by the time I shifted my eyes to that direction, I didn't see any birds. There were many roots sticking out on the ground, looking like stakes. The soil was wet, perhaps for the tides frequently washed onto the shore. There were no birds in the "paradise of the birds," I thought. The boat moved again, as a friend pushed the boat, and it drifted to the center of the river.

On the following day, we boated to a friend's hometown, the place we had seen the hills and the pagoda. Setting off from a little school, we passed the "paradise of the birds" again.

This time it was morning, and the sun was pouring over the water, as

A Paradise of Birds in Xinhui District in Jiangmen City.

well as the branches. Everything was extremely bright. We stopped under the tree for a moment.

It was very quiet at first, but then a burst of chirps broke the silence. We clapped our hands, and saw a big bird flying over, then a second, and a third. We continued to clap, and soon the woods became very boisterous. Bird chirps were all over the place, and so were the birds, the big ones, small ones, variegated ones and black ones. Some perched on the branches, chirping; some were flying up; some were flapping their wings.

I busied myself by watching them. Just as I saw this one clearly, I already missed the other one, and when I turned my eyes to the second one, the third one had flown off. A thrush flew out, but was startled by our clapping and then turned back into the woods. It stopped at a thin branch, and started to sing enthusiastically. The sounds were so beautiful.

As the boat was floating to the village under the pagoda, I kept turning back to look at the lush banyan left behind. I felt a little melancholy to leave this place. Yesterday, I was cheated by my eyes. The "paradise of the birds" is a real paradise for the birds!

---Ba Jin *The Paradise of Birds*

In 1933, one of the most famous writer in modern China, Ba Jin went sightseeing on the sandbank in the middle of Tianma River in Xinhui Area of Jiangmen City. There was a banyan with a history of more than 500 years on the islet. The branches of this tree dangled to the ground, some all the way into the soil, and became new roots. As time went on, the big banyan has grown into a forest in which thousands of birds inhabited. Ba Jin had some thoughts on such scenery and wrote down the essay — *The Paradise of Birds* which has been chosen into Chinese textbook for primary schools and become the spiritual memory of several generations of Chinese people.

49 years later, in 1982, Ba Jin again personally named this scenic spot "The Birds of Paradise". Since then, this name has been widely broadcasted in the world. Today, this place has already been the largest natural bird--watching park in the country and the famous international eco-attraction in Xinhui District.

Birds' paradise is the portrayal of the characteristics of Jiangmen. The birds suddenly appear and disappear but will not fly away from the sandbar, so do people.

Jiangmen is located at the confluence of the Xijiang River and its tributary Pengjiang River. Penglai Mountain and Yandun Mountain face each other like a door respectively on the northern and southern side of the Pengjiang River, thus "Jiangmen" is given the name.

Since ancient times Jiangmen has been the land of talents. "One family nourishes three academicians, and nine children are all talented". The nine children of the famous modern thinker Liang Qichao from Xinhui District in Jiangmen all become successful and have their own strengths.

Liang Qichao is recognized as an outstanding scholar in the late Qing

Dynasty, an encyclopedia–type person in Chinese history. Before the Revolution of 1911 which ends the rule of Qing Dynasty, in the debate with revolutionaries, he invented a new literary style, a style between the ancient Chinese and modern vernacular Chinese. Because it is easy to understand and flexible in syntax, it is very popular among people. Liang Qichao is the first person in China to use the term "Chinese nation" in articles.

There is one thing about him which is most known to Chinese people. In 1895, he, along with thousands of successful candidates in imperial examinations at the provincial level, submitted a joint letter to the Emperor Guangxu to fight against signing the "Treaty of Shimonoseki" which humiliates the country and forfeits its sovereignty after failing the Sino–Japanese War. This event is known as "Gongche Shangshu movement". Subsequently, supported by the emperor, he and his teacher Kang Youwei launched the Hundred Days Reform to advocate science and culture, reform political and educational system and develop agriculture, industry, business.

More than 100 days later, the movement failed, and most of the new policies were canceled. But the first national university in modern China, Imperial University of Peking, was kept. In 1912, Imperial University of Peking changed its name to Peking University. Peking University has always been one of the best universities in China.

Jiangmen locates in the western part of the Pearl River Delta. The five districts including Xinhui District (city), Kaiping County, Taishan County, Enping County and Heshan County under Jiangmen are well–known as "Wuyi" (the five counties) inside and outside the country, because the culture and customs of these five places are basically the same. In Jiangmen there are nearly 4 million overseas Chinese, ethnic Chinese, compatriots in Hong Kong and Macau, distributing over 107 countries and regions in five continents, 20% in Asia and 70% in the Americas.

In China, most famous hometowns of overseas Chinese are Jiangmen, Quanzhou, Chaoshan, Meizhou. Most of overseas Chinese from Quanzhou, Chaoshan and Meizhou are in Southeast Asia. Only overseas Chinese from Wuyi (five counties) are mainly distributed in the United States, Canada and Australia. It creates opportunities for Wuyi to promote cultural communications between China and foreign countries, in the meantime, preserves traditional Chinese culture. Traces of Sino–West blend can be found everywhere, from architecture, catering, clothing to customs.

One representative of overseas Chinese–Situ Meitang.

Situ Meitang is one of them.

On April 3, 1868, he was born in a farmer's family in Chikan Town, Kaiping County, Guangdong Province. In March 1880, only at the age of 12, Situ Meitang walked to Hong Kong from Kaiping and alone sailed to the United States by ferry.

In 1894, Situ Meitang came to Boston and set up On Leong Tong, advocating "fight for the weak against the strong, suppress the evil and pacify the good". On Leong Tong soon became a strong group owned by Chinese Freemasons, and finally spread over 31 cities in the United States, with large scale and more than 20,000 members. In 1905, Situ Meitang set up the general hall of On Leong Tong in New York, and the legal adviser was the later US president — Franklin Roosevelt.

Then Situ Meitang met Sun Yat–sen. When Sun Yat–sen launched movements in the United States, for protecting Sun Yat–sen, Situ Meitang accompanied him as a fulltime bodyguard and chef. In April 1911, after the Second Guangzhou Uprising failed, Tung Meng Hui was badly in need of 150,000 US dollars. Situ Meitang encouraged his fellows in Chinese Freemasons to donate. But he knew well that it was hard to collect such a huge amount of money in a short time merely relying on donation of overseas Chinese. In desperation, he put the four buildings of Chinese Freemasons in Toronto, Vancouver, Victoria and Jinshan Building in pawn. And later he sold a few buildings of Chinese Freemasons, scraped up the 150,000 US dollars, and supported armed uprisings. After the Wuchang Uprising took place in the same year, when Sun Yat–sen went back home from the United States, his travelling expenses were paid by Situ Meitang and others.

In 1932, the January 28 Incident broke out. The general Cai Tingkai led soldiers in the Nineteenth Route Army to bravely resist Japanese invaders. After news spread to the United States, Situ Meitang immediately organized donations and returned to the motherland with donations to comfort soldiers. He and Cai Tingkai also became close friends.

"Qiao" (overseas Chinese) is the"NDA"of Jiangmen city and the essential difference from other cities. Beginning in 2015, Jiangmen officially launched the construction of the capital of overseas Chinese, putting forward the need to polish the card of the capital of overseas China. Jiangmen also introduced the implemented the plan and action program for overseas Chinese business and city construction. At the end of 2016, Jiangmen put forward the requirement to vigorously develop global tourism, to build a strong tourism city, and to set up a special international travel destination in China. Kaiping City and Taishan City were confirmed as one of the units of national tourism demonstration areas.

The long "Chaoren Path" in the capital of overseas Chinese has become an important tool for the development of overseas Chinese affairs and tourism. "Chaoren Path" advocates measuring the prosper of the city by foot, connecting the existing roads, village roads, forest roads, climbing trails, country roads and other lines in series with nature protection areas, scenic spots, historical sites, ancient villages and rural scenery to form an urban and rural slow walking system, with characteristics of the hometown of overseas Chinese. In 2017, Jiangmen will construct the "Chaoren Path" with a total length of 3,000 kilometers. Over a period of time, "Chaoren Path" strives for a total length of 10,000 kilometers to create "the First Walking Path in Guangdong".

Centurial Diaolou and Overseas Chinese's Town

There is an old man whose family name is "Guan" in Chikan Town, Kaiping County. More than 30 of his relatives live in the United States and Canada. In Kaiping, the hometown of overseas Chinese, families like him can be found everywhere. It is said that Kaiping has a population of 650,000 people and 750,000 overseas relatives.

The famous Diaolou (the fortified multi–story tower) has recorded the rise and fall of a family of overseas Chinese, and maintained the love for the hometown and country rooted in the local and extended to the rest of the world. From gold mining and railway construction in North American, to the later rubber tapping and manor running in Southeast Asia, to the present emigration, Diaolou has witnessed stories of generation after generation who made a long and difficult journey to realize their dreams.

The architecture in the hometown of overseas Chinese in Wuyi fully integrates with the characteristics of Western

Jiangmen Diaolou. Photographer: Chen Jie

architecture, among which, Kaiping Diaolou is the most famous and most special one. Kaiping Diaolou, combining traditional Chinese architectural culture with the uniqueness of Western architectural culture, has become a monument to the memory of overseas Chinese culture and reflected the course of overseas Chinese and Chinese people's initiative acceptance of Western culture.

The amount of Kaiping Diaolou is more than 1,800. In 2007, "Kaiping Diaolou and Villages" was officially listed on the World Heritage List, becoming the 35th world heritage in China. Thus, the first world heritage project of overseas Chinese culture was born in China.

World Heritage Committee evaluates Guangdong Kaiping Diaolou like this: Kaiping Diaolou are multi−storeyed defensive village houses in Kaiping. Retaining a harmonious relationship with the surrounding landscape, Kaiping Diaolou display a complex and flamboyant fusion of Chinese and Western structural and decorative forms.

After Ming Dynasty, in Jiangmen area, bandits were rampant and social security was in chaos. Additionally, there were many rivers in this area. When there were typhoon rainstorms, flood disaster frequently occurred. Clever Jiangmen people chose to build fortified multi−story towers in the village for protection.

In the 1920s, Diaolou ushered in the peak period of its construction. Overseas Chinese who had lived abroad for decades returned home with their savings and built multi−storeyed defensive towers one after another to protect their families and properties.

Kaiping Diaolou are multi−storeyed buildings, higher than ordinary houses, which makes it convenient for condescending defense. Walls of the towers are thicker than the ordinary houses. So, residents in Kaiping are not afraid of robbers' chiseling holes in the walls or fire attack. The towers have smaller windows than the ordinary houses. Many windows are equipped with iron gratings and sashes as well as iron plates outwards. The upper four corners of towers are generally equipped with total−closed or semi−closed hornworks (commonly known as "swallow nests") which reach out of cantilevers. Inside every hornwork there are forward and downward shooting holes, through which you can shoot at village invaders in a higher position. At the same time, on each wall of every story there are shooting holes, increasing the number of attack points for residents.

Kaiping Diaolou have different usages, resulting in different classifications: the public tower, the living tower and the watchtower.

Villagers or some families raise money to build living towers at the back of the village. One family gets one room to avoid bandits or floods. Living towers are also built at the back of the village by wealthy people. With large space and fully equipped living facilities, living towers have two functions: defense and living. Watchtowers are mainly built at the gate of the village or hills and riversides outside the village. Many watchtowers are equipped with searchlights and alarms, which makes it easy for villagers to find out bandits in advance and warn villagers in other villages.

The upper part of Kaiping Diaolou is most expressive. People mainly make use of the dome, mountain flower, order and other architectural elements which appear in foreign buildings, forming thousands of architectural styles. Different architectural styles reflect the different economic strength of the landlord, aesthetic taste and the extent of the impact of foreign architectural culture.

The Diaolou cluster located in Zili Village, Tangkou Town, Kaiping County is one of the world cultural heritage sites. It became famous because it is the place where Chinese film *Let the Bullets Fly* was shot. *Let the Bullets Fly* is a film released in 2010 and set in in southern China during the warring 1920s. After ambushing a government horse train, the leading bandit Zhang Muzhi came across a big liar Lao Tang. They develop from enemies to close friends. However, the real battle has just begun. Huang Silang, the mobster boss in southern China, casts greedy eyes on Goose Town. A series of breathtaking battles are put on stage one after another.

In 2017, the total number of Chinese cinema screens has been more than 40,000. China has become a country with most cinema screens in the world. Chinese movies seem to usher in the best of times, but real impressive movies are rare. The film *Let the Bullets Fly* is considered as one of the films worth recording in this era.

Let the Bullets Fly is directed and starred by Jiang Wen, one of the

In Zili Village, there are 15 towers with different styles, delicate shapes and rich connotations, which are outstanding representatives of Kaiping Diaolou in the flourishing period. Photographer: Chen Jie

most important figures in contemporary Chinese film industry. It is his fourth film.

Yunhuan Tower is one of the 15 towers in Zili Village. In 1921, Yunhuan Tower was built with an area of 80 square meters.

This year, China was still seeking an independent and prosperous road. For Chinese people, this year the most important thing is that the first national congress of the Communist Party of China was held in Shanghai and the Communist Party of China was born. 28 years later, the Chinese Communist Party became China's ruling party and founded the People's Republic of China.

The constructor of Huanyun Tower Fang Wenxian had lived in Malaysia and was enthusiastic about public welfare. In 1918, Fang Wenxian donated 5000 yuan and raised 17000 yuan for building Qiangya School in his hometown. During Japanese invasion of China, he donated money for the resistance against Japanese invasion and purchased liberty bonds.

He built this tower out of consideration of reverting to his origin. The external style and decoration of the five-storied Yunhuan Tower has some characteristics of the Western style. But inside the tower, Fang Wenxian' and his families' living utensils are still preserved, showing an image of traditional rural home furnishings in southern China.

He also personally wrote a couplet for the tower: "云龙风虎际会常怀怎奈壮志莫愁只赢得湖海生涯空山岁月　幻影昙花身世如梦何妨豪情自放无负此阳春烟景大块文章".

The couplet is expressed that: they often have a big career desire, but unfortunately the ambition is difficult to achieve, can only wander rivers and lakes, helpless wasted years; although everything is like phantom, there is still a need to express lofty sentiments to live up to the present beautiful spring scenery and splendid articles.

In Chinese culture, a couplet should have a horizontal scroll. The horizontal scroll of the couplet is "only talking about personal sentiments". The businessman present his love for his country and his hometown as well as his resentment and depression towards turbulent times in the couplet.

Not only towers, in Kaiping country, there are some villages whose name is deeply marked with the "Qiao" (overseas Chinese). The emergence and construction of these villages is a miniature of the immigrant history of hometowns of overseas Chinese, behind which is written the struggling entrepreneurial spirit as well as patriotic feeling of overseas Chinese.

Speaking of buildings overseas Chinese villages, people will be surprised with constructors' particular selection of building materials. Some of building materials needed to build luxury houses were directly purchased overseas. "Canadian Village" was designed by hiring Canadian

Canadian Village. Photographer: Chen Jie

designers who brought the construction drawings of villages and villas back home, and with the combination of Chinese and Western cultural elements. The steels, cement and wood needed to construct villas were also shipped from Canada to Hong Kong and then to Kaiping by Canadian overseas Chinese, which took three months.

Walking into the "Burmese Village", you will see 12 two-storied high houses arranged in two rows, neatly located in the fields. In front of the village is the open ground, and outside the village is the pond. The distance between houses are "equidistant", about 2 meters wide. The roofs are the hard summit-type structure of pad surface; walls are built up with black bricks; stairs and doors are made teakwood; beams are shaped like the Chinese character "Gong" and built with iron and teakwood.

Most of these houses are with two rooms, two corridors and one hall, and a few houses are with one room and one gallery. The needed teakwood is purchased from Burma; cement and steel is transported back from Hong Kong by hiring ships. The constructor of the village is Xu Suixing. To make a living, he went to Burma with his brother Xu Chunxing, and did odds and ends in a wood factory. Because of working hard, a few years later, they had a certain savings, and set up a wood factory named “Wang Xing Long”. In its heyday, the shops run by him are up to dozens. He became a well–known local businessman. Although their days in Burma were quite comfortable, the two still inevitably missed their home, so they afterwards returned home to build houses.

Sprouted Overseas, Rooted in Jiangmen

"Dad goes to San Francisco, soon send money back, the whole family rely on you, to send money back." This is a ballad familiarized by overseas Chinese whose ancestral home is in Jiangmen. In old China, a lot of Chinese people were abducted to labor in foreign countries as "piglets". They travelled far away across the sea to San Francisco in the United States, and then washed mineral sands, did hard manual work and participated in the construction of the US Central Pacific Railway. 80% of the Chinese railway constructors came from Jiangmen. Too many people passed away in a foreign country.

An article entitled *Overseas Chinese Deep Love for Jiangmen* introduces that when Sun Yat–sen led the Revolution of 1911, established "Revive China Society", "Tung Meng Hui" and the KMT, Jiangmen overseas Chinese enthusiastically participated. Sun Yat–sen organized armed uprisings 10 times, and funds needed were afforded by overseas Chinese, among whom Jiangmen overseas Chinese made the greatest contributions. He once said

Jiangmen Wuyi Overseas Chinese Museum intensively displays historical culture, customs, economic development, social progress and folk art of the hometown of overseas Chinese, including the literature and relics about the migration of overseas Chinese as well as various kinds of typical working tools and living appliances once used by overseas Chinese at home and abroad, and some of them are of great value. The picture is a statue in the museum, showing that Chinese labors are constructing the American Western Railway. Photographer: Chen Jie

that "overseas Chinese as the mother of revolution", which indicates overseas Chinese great contributions to the revolution.

From 1937 to August 1945, Jiangmen overseas Chinese donations in the United States reached more than 56 million US dollars. At that time the National Government issued nation-saving government bonds six times with a total value of 3 billion yuan, of which Jiangmen overseas Chinese subscribed for 1.11 billion yuan.

In 2010, Jiangmen Wuyi Overseas Chinese Museum was fully open to the public. More than 40,000 pieces of collections of overseas Chinese in the museum faithfully and fully record this phase of history, tell touching stories about Wuyi overseas Chinese who start their business abroad and make contributions to their hometown.

Chen Yixi, a villager in Meitang Village, Liu Village, Doushan Town, Taishan City, born in 1844, went to America at the age of 11, then participated in the US railway construction and became a railway engineer. And then he was engaged in business, running operating "Guang De Hao", participated in many construction projects in Seattle and became an influential Chinese businessman. During the period of US exclusion of Chinese, Chen Yixi defied brutal suppression, actively fought for Chinese rights and interests as well as united and organized people to resist against suppressions. He was admired and loved by overseas Chinese, becoming an influential leader of overseas Chinese.

At the age of 60, Chen Yuxi gave up superior living conditions in the United States, came back his poor hometown, led the villagers to build a railway of Chinese people—Sunning Railway. The construction of Sunning Railway was without any participation of foreign loans, foreign stocks and foreign workers. It was constructed on Chinese own, from the preparation, design, construction, operation to management, which set a new trend. He was determined to "construct a railway of Chinese own by using Chinese capital, to make outstanding achievements by virtue of Chinese strength".

The construction of Sunning railway was officially started on May 1, 1906 and completed on March 30, 1920, which lasts 14 years. The railway has a total length of 133 kilometers and includes 46 stations, 215 bridges and 236 culverts. In addition, a large number of projects such as Gongyi Terminal, Beijie Terminal, Gongyi Machine Factory and Niuwan Shipping Company were completed one after another. What's more, "turntables" and "train ferries" are pioneering achievements in Chinese railroad history, establishing a land and water transport network with Taicheng as a transportation hub and Sunning Railway as the main line. This transport network has become the main artery of the social and economic development of Jiangmen Wuyi in the Republic of China era.

In 1933, Bajin took a train ferry on Sunning railway passing through the Tangjiang River and wrote down the famous prose "The Poem of Machine".

He wrote: "In order to see a friend, I became a passenger on Sunning Railway. My three friends and I spent about three hours on the train all the way from Huicheng to Gongyi. Despite of long time and hot weather, I did not feel lonely.

The scenery in the South was indeed enchanting. In my eyes, everything was beautiful like a dream: lush green trees, bright red soil, pieces of rice fields, piles of houses, the mirror–like river and lofty towers. Although the countryside in the South contained a lot of pain, on the surface they were still very calm and very beautiful! Arriving Tanjiang, the train stopped. The wheels did not move; however, the outside scenery began to move slowly. This is not a miracle. This is the most beautiful project on the Sunning Railway. "

Sunning Railway has been run around for 30 years. During the Anti–Japanese War, it was severely damaged by Japanese troops, then the National Government ordered to demolish it, and only the site of Beijing Railway Station was left until now.

Based on data, overseas Chinese, ethnic Chinese as well as Hong Kong, Macao and Taiwan compatriots whose ancestral home are Jiangmen are nearly 4 million, spreading all over 107 countries and regions in the world. The population of overseas Chinese and ethnic Chinese is the basically equal with the population of Jiangmen City. So, there is a saying about Jiangmen: "two Jiangmen respectively at home and abroad".

Political figures, such as the former American Ambassador to China Gary Faye Locke, the Mayor of San Francisco Edwin Mah Lee, the Mayor of Auckland City Jean Quan, the Chief Executive of the Macao Special Administrative Region Fernando Chui as well as Hong Kong stars such as Andy Lau, Chow Yun Fat, Alan Tam, Tony Leung and Donnie Yen are all rooted in Jiangmen.

Overseas Chinese love their country and hometown. They make contributions to the development of their hometown by means of donation and investment. By the end of 2015, their donations for their hometown were up to 7.26 billion Hong Kong dollars, and the investment amounted to 20.22 billion US dollars. Jiangmen specially set up the "honorary citizen" award system to commend overseas Chinese, foreigners and domestic people who have made outstanding contributions in promoting the civilized development of charitable and public service, friendly foreign exchanges as well as economic and technological development in Jiangmen. Since 1993, eight batches of 700 people at home and abroad have been dubbed "Honorary Citizens of Jiangmen City".

Huang Xiaojuan is an honorary citizen of Jiangmen City. She grew up in Sabah, Malaysia, and studied in Canada in her early years. After graduating from college, she followed his father to do real estate business, and step by step became a famous female entrepreneur in Sabah.

Huang Xiaojuan's father has donated more than 100 million yuan for the reconstruction of playgrounds and teaching buildings in local schools in Taishan. Huang Xiaojuan remembers that since 1980, her father has returned home every year to visit relatives. In 1998, Huang Xiaojuan paid her first visit to Taishan, and after hearing that some primary schools need to be repaired, she immediately contacted with these schools.

For Huang Xiaojuan, it is a kind of honor and responsibility to become a bridge linking together the economy, trade and culture of Jiangmen and Sabah.

Outstanding overseas Chinese with family ties in Jiangmen should also include Julie Fong. At the 36th Grammy Awards in 1994, by virtue of Ten Summoner's Tales, Julie Fong won the trophy of the best music production. This is the first time for a Chinese to stand on the podium of the Grammy Award.

Born in 1964 in San Francisco, Julie Fong, whose ancestral home is in Shangtang Village, Qiangya Village Committee, Tangkou Town, Kaiping City, Guangdong Province, is the second generation of Chinese. Her father Fang Chuangjie is a well–known overseas Chinese leader. In the 1950s, he founded an insurance bank named after his own name in San Francisco. In university Julie Fong tried film and television production, and after graduation she produced music videos.

In recognition of Julie Fong's achievements, on July 16, 1994, in addition to the award, the Mayor's office of San Francisco declared the day of 16th as "Julie Fong Day".

广州：古港新作为

黄埔古港的前世今生

2015年12月，广东省会广州，这个1300多万人口的大都市，正在广州博物馆举行“哥德堡号”瓷器展览。这近百件瓷器出发于1745年的广州，却在瑞典的哥德堡（Goteborg）港海底沉睡200多年。用中国人的话说，它这算是“回娘家”。

1745年1月11日，瑞典商船“哥德堡号”从广州启程回国，船上装载着大约700吨在广州采购的中国货物，包括366吨茶叶、50万~70万件瓷器，还有丝绸、藤器和珍珠母等。这是它第三次来广州，也是最后一次。

1757年清朝政府宣布实行“一口通商”，各国来中国贸易都要来到广州，也只能来到广州。

这一年，按中国的旧历是清乾隆二十二年。乾隆是当时中国最高统治者爱新觉罗·弘历皇帝的年号。中国古代新皇登基，为了区别前任（多数是自己的父亲），会设置一个年号，用于计算年份。乾隆二十二年就是弘历当上皇帝的第二十二个年头。

乾隆，寓意“天道昌隆”，事实也正如此。乾隆是中国古代寿命最长的一个皇帝，他活了88岁。从他的爷爷康熙皇帝（这位是最受中国人欣赏的古代最高统治者之一），到他的父亲雍正皇帝，再到乾隆皇帝，是中国历史上文化、经济、手工业极盛的时代。在中国，对一个朝代最大的褒奖就是被称为盛世——在很长时间内保持繁荣昌盛——这三位皇帝缔造了中国的“康乾盛世”。

“康乾盛世”中“乾”字所代表的皇帝就是乾隆。乾隆自称“十全老人”，“十全”表示没有欠缺，可见这位皇上的自信。他还是中国写过最多古诗的人，据说是3万多首，即使唐宋诗词巅峰时的那些伟大诗人也无法与他相比。

“一口通商”35年后，1792年英国派马嘎尔尼率船队以为乾隆补祝八十大寿的名义来到了中国，按规定藩属国见皇帝都要下跪，双方在是否下跪以及怎样下跪上进行了事关尊严和国体但实际上更是文化隔阂的争议。后世的人会认为，这实际上是中国从开放走向封闭的象征。

航行8个月后，“哥德堡号”来到离哥德堡港大约900米的海面，离家30个月的船员们已能看到自己的故乡，然而就在这个时候，船头触礁随即沉没，正在岸上等待凯旋的人们只好眼睁睁地目睹船沉到海里。幸运的是，所有船员安然无恙。

大约1/3的货物被打捞出来，在市场上出售所得除了支付这次广州之旅的全部成本外，竟然还能获利14%。“哥德堡号”和船上2/3的货物长眠海底，默默等待着200多年后重见天日的那一刻。

1984年，瑞典一次民间考古活动发现了“哥德堡号”残骸。两年后，开始考古发掘。很快，就打捞出400多件完整的瓷器和9吨重的瓷器碎片，这些瓷器大部分具有中国传统的图案花纹，少量绘有欧洲特色图案，显然是当年“哥德堡号”为特定客户专门订购的

“订烧瓷”。

当“哥德堡号”再次来到广州时，已是150年后的2009年。不过，这次是仿制旧船而造的新船，按照中国人的习惯，称它为“哥德堡三号”。

它耗费了4000名工匠的十年时间，当然还有3000万美元。

广州为迎接这位“新朋友”，斥巨资在黄埔古港和南海神庙重建了两个码头，码头及其周边都以古代样式为蓝本，复原200多年前的景象。他们希望展示以海上丝绸之路为代表的中国海洋文化，展现广州的贸易历史，再塑千年古港的世界声誉。

“哥德堡三号”航行路线也按古时安排，这是16世纪前全世界最长的一条航线。一切很顺利，但到达广州花了它300多天的时间，航程约为3700公里。

瑞典国王卡尔16世古斯塔夫和西尔维亚王后同船抵达。据说，把广州选为“哥德堡三号”到中国后的第一个城市，是国王本人的要求。广州人没有辜负瑞典人的厚谊，参观者络绎不绝。

新锐杂志《新周刊》这样评价“哥德堡三号”来到广州：两个国家的两座城市，用一艘仿古帆船，一条古代商贸航线，上演了一场有200多年历史内涵的好戏。中央电视台把这个创举录进了《探索与发现》栏目，广州人把它视为“花多少钱也买不来的宣传广州的大好机会”，瑞典人把复航计划变成一次极具创意的“文化形象工程”。“哥德堡号”的重生，展示了一个值得借鉴的公关模式，它既是赞助商的市场公关，也是国家的经贸公关，更是民族的文化公关。

“哥德堡三号”连接的是广州对外交往的历史与未来。到广州后，它还是像1857年那样，停泊在黄埔古港——一个1500年从未与外界失去联系，即便在清末闭关锁国时依旧顽强生存的“一口通商”之地。

“凡载洋货入口之外国商船，不得沿江湾泊，必须下锚于黄埔”。黄埔，就是黄埔古港。从1758年至1837年的80年间，停泊在黄埔古港的外国商船共计5107艘。作为相当长一段时间内中国唯一的港口，它见证了广州“海上丝绸之路”的繁荣，迎接了包括美国的“中国皇后号”、俄罗斯的“希望号”等外国商船，特别是“中国皇后号”的访华，打开了中美贸易的大门。

中国历史学家黄仁宇在其著作《万历十五年》中，从大历史的角度提出中国在近代化的过程中落后，无关道德和个人因素，而是在技术上不能实现“数目字管理”。但在有些数字上，其实中国人做得不错，比如关于这5107艘船的统计。

在中国伟大的史学家、文学家、思想家司马迁笔下，广州是“珠玑、犀、瑇瑁、果、布之凑”的大都会。黄埔古港位于现在的广州市海珠区新港东路。它所在的黄埔村，仍是一派古朴景色。渡口旁的大榕树斜横，芭蕉林悦眼，渔船点点，不过已鲜见商贸的痕迹。

黄埔村原村名为“凤浦”，村南紧靠珠江就有一座刻有“凤浦”二字的彩牌坊。相传古时有一对凤凰飞临此地，从此人丁兴旺，五谷丰登。传说终归会是美好而吉祥的。

该村地处一小岛，在中国水边地区叫“浦”，水中的陆地曰“洲”，所以取村名为“凰洲”或“凤浦”，后演变成为“黄埔”之名。

村中保留的大量遗迹和文物，见证了“古代海上丝绸之路”的世代繁盛，证明了黄埔古港独一无二的历史地位，也反映了广州沧海桑田的巨大变迁。黄埔村就是一座“古代海上丝绸之路”活的博物馆，因为最有价值的历史就存在于当下人们的内心。

黄埔古港兴旺发达时，正是17世纪到19世纪广州海外贸易鼎盛期，也就是近代西方商人津津乐道的“对华贸易的黄金时代”。英国人威廉·希克1769年来过广州，他对广州赞不绝口：“珠江上船舶运行穿梭的情景，就像伦敦桥下泰晤士河，不同的是，河面的帆船形式不同，还有大帆船，在外国人眼里再没有比排列在长达几里的帆船更为壮观的了。”

有人这样评价，处于东方海岸之边的广州黄埔古港，一艘艘大船从这里启程，扬帆远航，将丝绸、瓷器、茶叶带往世界各地的同时，也带去了农耕及手工业技术、造纸术和指南针，搭乘商船来来往往的高僧、科学家、画师、译者更是文化交融的使者。从这个意义上说，在持续千年的历史长河中，作为海上丝绸之路发祥地之一的广州，是中华文明影响世界之旅的一大启程地。

历史已经远去，昔日的辉煌逐渐消失在慢慢淤积的古港渡口，码头也看不到昔日的忙碌和繁华。历史需要记忆的承载，建设一个黄埔古港历史陈列馆是个不错的主意，广州人也这样做了。

黄埔古港历史陈列馆利用村内的一个祠堂改造而成，2000平米的面积由“古港遗韵”壁画区、“扶胥生辉”实物区以及中心展区三部分组成。其中，实物区是陈列馆最有特色的部分。设计人员将四散在黄埔古村内的40多件历代建筑材料，如石梁、石柱、石刻等集中在一起，在院落中营造出一个“残垣断壁”的景区。他们没有选择把这些文物围起来展出，是希望让游客能够近距离地感受古港文化的辉煌。

在展馆的壁画区内，横亘着一幅长31米、高1.5米的大型汉白玉描金壁画。画内描绘了黄埔古港“一港通商”时期万船来埠的繁荣景象，“歌德堡号”“中国皇后号”都位列其中。这幅壁画应该是在一些外国人写生留下的图画的基础上设计而成。

黄埔古港作为中国重要的对外港口，船舶云集，经济繁荣，村民也较早接触外国人及外来文化，不少人外出留学、经商，名人辈出。有清政府、日本、俄国驻新加坡的三国领事胡璇泽，有留美学生、向美国总统索回多付赔款以建清华大学的梁诚，有为护送孙中山脱险拖延病情不治的冯肇宪，还有铁路专家胡栋朝、农业专家冯锐、经济学家梁方仲。

黄埔村还有个保护一方免受日本军侵略谜一般的日本媳妇的故事，颇具传奇色彩。

1900年，黄埔村村民冯佐屏前往日本求学，认识了一位日本姑娘。二人不久结为夫妻。1924年，40多岁的冯佐屏为侍奉父母，加上思乡情浓，携家人从日本归来，回黄埔村定居。

为解妻子的思乡之苦，冯佐屏兴建了一栋日式风格的小洋楼送给妻子，使她能安心居住下来。这就是如今坐落在黄埔村惇慵街8号的“日本楼”。

日本发动侵华战争后广州沦陷，一队日军来到黄埔村，眼看村民即将遭受屠戮。突然，冯佐屏的妻子出现在日军面前，亮出了一把宝刀。日军见刀后放下军刀，崇敬地向刀拜了拜，然后退出了黄埔村。抗战期间，日军从未到黄埔村扫荡。

附近村庄的村民得知日军不敢进黄埔村，便纷纷躲进黄埔村避难。因此，黄埔村又被称之为“平安村”。1944年，冯佐屏的妻子生病过世，葬于黄埔村内山顶。

关于这把刀的来历，在黄埔村流行三种说法。一据说冯妻是日本天皇一位远亲，这把刀是她的嫁妆；二据说她是日本幕府末年将军的侄女，宝刀是将军赠予的；第三种说法是她是当年某位首相的侄女，刀由他相赠。

熟知村史的一位老人家更认同第三种说法。“日本是等级森严的国家，如果她是皇族或是幕府将军的亲戚，是不可能下嫁异族或平民的。”不管怎样，日本媳妇对黄埔村的贡献是实实在在的。

2000年长盛不衰

“哥德堡号”是在历经艰辛即将到家时“功亏一篑”，而另外一艘中国人更为熟悉的“南海一号”则是离开中国泉州港不久后就沉于海底。

泉州是中国古代的另一个重要港口，唐朝时为世界四大口岸之一，宋元时期为“东方第一大港”，被马可·波罗誉为“光明之城”。马可·波罗可能是为数不多的在中国比在本国更为知名的意大利人。他在《马可·波罗游记》中描述了他在中国的见闻，激起了欧洲人对东方的热烈向往，对以后新航路的开辟产生了巨大的影响。不过，很多人怀疑他对中国的描绘有时稍显夸张。

与“哥德堡号”只能供后人想象不同，见证海上丝绸之路历史的“南海一号”则因整体挖掘而能让我们睹其真颜。

1987年，在广东南部的阳江海域，发现一个距今800多年的沉船遗址。这个后来被称为“南海一号”的家伙，是迄今为止世界上发现的海上沉船中年代最早、船体最大、保存最完整的远洋贸易商船。据估算，它的长度达到30.4米、宽9.8米，船身（不算桅杆）高约4米，排水量达到600吨以上，载重近800吨。事实上，我们并不知道这艘船本来的名字，也许本就没有名字。

“南海一号”在泉州港口装货后，也许是遭遇风暴，也许是船底漏水，或是我们不知道的其他原因，最终沉没海底。对它的打捞，却已是发现它整整20年后，并且创造性地使用“整体打捞”的方案，将沉船、文物与其周围海水、泥沙按照原状一次性吊浮起运，迁移到广东海上丝绸之路博物馆内，再进行文物整理。

没人不关心“南海一号”里到底有什么宝贝。2016年1月5日，总共出土文物14000余件套、标本2575件，其中瓷器13000余件套、金器151件套、银器124件套、铜器170件，铜钱约17000枚以及大量动植物标本、船木等。

“南海一号”正处在古代海上丝绸之路的航道上。海上丝绸之路是古代连接东西方海道的交通大动脉，因运送的主要大宗货物是丝绸，所以被叫做海上丝绸之路。随着运送货物的变化，它也曾被叫做“海上陶瓷之路”“海上香料之路”。它从中国东南沿海，经过中南半岛和南海诸国，穿过印度洋，进入红海，抵达东非和欧洲。中宋元时期，中国同世界60多个国家有着直接的“海上丝路”商贸往来。明代郑和下西洋的成功，海上丝绸之路发展到极盛时期。

尽管繁荣异常，但在相当长的一段时间内，海上丝绸之路只是存在于零星的文献记载中，人们对它知之甚少。直到20世纪，在航线沿岸港口陆续发现来自中国的瓷器、丝绸等文物，海上丝绸之路的面目才逐渐清晰起来。“南海一号”能为这段历史的研究提供可信的模本，复原和填补与之相关的一段历史空白，甚至展现文献和陆上考古无法提供的信息。

中国境内海上丝绸之路主要有广州、泉州、宁波三个主港和扬州、福州等其他支线港组成。广州从3世纪30年代起，就是海上丝绸之路的主港。它被称为世界海上交通史上唯一2000多年长盛不衰的大港。

2015年，中国正式提出“一带一路”（The Belt and Road，缩写B&R）倡议，这是“丝绸之路经济带”和“21世纪海上丝绸之路”的简称。它将充分依靠中国与有关国家既有的双多边机制，借助既有的、行之有效的区域合作平台，借用古代丝绸之路的历史符号，高举和平发展的旗帜，积极发展与沿线国家的经济合作伙伴关系，共同打造政治互信、经济融合、文化包容的利益共同体、命运共同体和责任共同体。

广州的“伸展”运动

19世纪时，中美贸易几乎都在商行之间进行交易。一个名叫伍秉鉴的商人，他的商行在美国久负盛名，生意几近垄断。不过，比起他的真名，商名浩官（Howqua）更为美国商人所熟知，Hu-Kwa Tea也是因此得名。

2014年，康涅狄格大学副教授、福布斯博物馆董事罗伯特·福布斯，在祖辈留下的位于波士顿米尔顿区（Milton）的祖屋，办了美国第一家中美贸易博物馆（Forbes House Museum）。这家博物馆，面积不大，但完好地保存了祖辈从广州带回来的每一件物品。

罗伯特·福布斯的高曾祖父也叫罗伯特·福布斯（Robert Forbes），13岁时他乘坐一艘商船漂洋过海历经艰辛来到广州，投奔开商行的舅舅学做生意。他和伍秉鉴交往密切。离开广州时，伍秉鉴赠送一幅自画像以为留念。罗伯特·福布斯就是听着这些往事，看着精心保存的中国画像、瓷器慢慢长大的。

伍秉鉴的父亲伍国莹从事对外贸易，并在1783年成立了怡和行。伍秉鉴生于1769年，32岁接手怡和行后，伍家事业快速崛起。大约在他60岁时，他和他的家族拥有的财产高达2600万银元。他们不但在国内拥有地产、房产、茶山、店铺和巨款，而且在美国投资铁路、证券交易和保险业务，怡和行成为名副其实的跨国财团。

2001年，《华尔街日报》专门统计了1000年来世界上最富有的50个人。其中6个入选的中国人是成吉思汗、忽必烈、刘瑾、和珅、伍秉鉴和宋子文。《华尔街日报》评价说："出生于1769年的清朝行商伍秉鉴继承父业与外商从事买卖，又进一步贷款给外商并以此获得巨额财富。他在西方商界享有相当高的知名度。"

伍秉鉴被西方商人认为"诚实、亲切、细心、慷慨，而且富有"，英国人称赞他"善于理财，聪明过人"。据说，伍秉鉴经营理念超前，与欧美各国重要客户建立了紧密联系。流传很广的一个故事是，一个美国商人因经营不善，欠了伍秉鉴七万多美元的债务无力偿还。伍秉鉴得知后，把借据撕碎，宣布账目结清，使这位商人得以重返家园。伍秉鉴应该深谙"商标"的重要性，他将自己的肖像附送在销往海外的茶叶中。尽管这个样貌清瘦的生意人一生没离开过广州，但他的肖像却随着货物走到美洲、英国以及印度。

这位晚清的大生意人，一度是广州十三行的首富，怡和行也成为广州十三行发展的缩影。十三行是官府特许经营对外贸易商行的总称，并不必然是十三个商行。

广州"一口通商"后，十三行的商人在80多年的时间里，成为大清帝国对外的唯一管家。除了做生意之外，来华洋商从货物买卖到日常起居，事无巨细，都必须通过十三行才能办理。

不过，《南京条约》规定开放广州、厦门、福州、宁波、上海五处为通商口岸（史称"五口通商"）。十三行不再拥有独揽中国对外贸易的特权，也就日趋没落。

十三行曾是广州的商业中心。它所在的附近区域，包括北京路区域在内，一直是近代以前广州城的行政中心，广府文化的中心，也是历史上最繁华的商业集散地。

直到改革开放后，以北京路商圈为核心的老城区中心商业轴和以天河城商圈为核心的新城市中轴线商务发展轴，成为广州城市和经济发展双动力。

广州的变化如此之快。曾经“不到南方大厦，不算到了广州”的城市地标，到后来的北京路步行街、天河路商圈，再到如今的珠江新城，城市中心的变迁，见证着广州城市的发展。2004年，广州天河区成为新城市中心区。

2010年，广州亚运会开幕式在珠江上一个名叫海心沙的小岛上举行，海心沙就在这所城市的新中轴线上。有人说，这里集中了太多的广州之最——最高的摩天大楼、最大的市民广场、最大的地下空间、最好的文化建筑以及最繁华的中央商务区。

广交会的开放基因

广州的“伸展”运动，不仅在于城市的扩张，更在于以开放的心态面向世界，这是深藏在这个城市骨髓里的基因，也是这个城市独特的精神气质。这集中地体现在广交会上。

1957年，中国出口商品交易会在广州诞生，这个更被人习惯地称为广交会的展会，开辟了一条中国与世界交往的通道，它是历史最长、层次最高、规模最大、商品种类最齐全、到会境外采购商最多、成交效果最好的“中国第一展”。

为什么要把第一个全国出口商品的展览会放在广州举办？自有其不为外人所知的原因。广州作为千年商都，商业氛围浓厚，地域优势独特，是香港、澳门地区以及东南亚商人到中国内地做生意的唯一通道。

20世纪70年代初，广交会在流花路的新展馆启用。流花展馆与广州火车站近在咫尺，五六公里车程之外就是白云机场（不过现在它已搬到离市中心更远的郊区，为示区别，被叫做新白云机场）。1986年，流花路展馆与周围的东方宾馆新楼、流花宾馆、广州市新火车站等现代建筑群，被评为羊城新八景之一——“流花玉宇”。

羊在中国的文化里是驯顺的代表，因与“阳”同音，有吉祥之意。广州因与羊有关的一个传说，又被称为“羊城”。从宋代开始，这个城市的人们就不断评选城市的八种名胜景点，称作“羊城八景”。

2001年4月，在距离流花展馆十多公里的东部琶洲，开始建设新的会展中心，并在2003年使用。2008年10月，第104届广交会就已全部在琶洲展馆举行。

琶洲，这个黄埔古港所在的地方，利用琶洲会展中心，再次成为广州向世界敞开交流之门的象征。

互联网时代的到来，广交会也在不断推陈出新，它搭建电商平台，打造全年365天不落幕的网上广交会。广交会拥抱互联网，琶洲也热烈拥抱互联网，琶洲岛西侧的互联网创新集聚区，聚集了腾讯、阿里巴巴、小米、唯品会等几十家企业，设立总部或项目公司。

其中就包括微信。微信所在的公司名叫腾讯。在微信以前，他们的社交软件QQ一度是最受欢迎的。也许这是一种展示企业雄心的方式，腾讯以17.6亿元获得琶洲的一块地以建设微信总部大楼。

相信即便在多年以后，中国人也会记得在这个时代有一款名叫微信的社交软件，深刻影响着中国人的日常生活。它以“连接一切”作为口号，成为这个时代绝大多数中国人智能手机里必会安装的一款软件。在相当长的一段时间里，它让很多中国人的钱包里不用装现金，因为在线支付已是如此普及，你在中国偏僻农村的一个小商店里，也可以通过扫一个名叫二维码的东西直接付款。整个交易过程，无需使用现金。

2016年第二季度，微信已经覆盖中国94%以上的智能手机，月活跃用户达到8.06亿，用户覆盖200多个国家、超过20种语言。

微信就诞生在广州。它用一种特别的方式让中国与世界连接，让世界变得更为开放。

微信和QQ所在只是腾讯公司最具代表性的产品。这家公司的实际负责人马化腾，最初创业时率领自己的团队做网页、做系统集成、做程序设计。但由于不懂市场和市场运作，产品拿出去向运营商推销，却经常被拒之门外。这种经历，相信不管是比尔盖茨还是乔布斯，应该都曾体会过。

2016年10月，中国移动互联网用户总数已经达到10.77亿，使用手机上网的用户数再创历史新高，总数达到了10.2亿，这在全球首屈一指。人们把互联网的体验从早前的桌面PC带到了工作生活的方方面面，各个领域都可以永远在线、实时在线，给所有行业借助微信的力量发展线上线下业务提供了良好基础，意味着很多的机会。而微信以及与它同类的产品会给中国带来的改变，还在进行中，远远没有结束。

自贸区：对接世界的“焊点”

以南沙为中心，以50公里为半径画一个圆，可囊括珠三角所有重要城市，包括香港和澳门所有港口码头。以100公里为半径覆盖珠三角9座城市和5大国际机场。在地理上，南沙就是珠三角的中心。但它远远不是经济的发展中心。在“发展是硬道理”的中国，南沙却似乎验证了中国的一句俗语“灯下黑”——虽处中心却被有意无意忽略。以至于20世纪80年代，一片荒滩的南沙，被称为广州的“西伯利亚”，荒凉而缺少生气。

但霍英东不这样看。这是一位香港的实业家，以驳运起家，后从事房地产，他首创了后来通行全国的分期付款模式。2006年他逝世时，官方通告说他是“中国共产党的亲密朋友”，在中国人的眼中，他是值得信赖的爱国人士。像诸多香港人一样，霍英东祖籍也在广东。他曾为家乡广州番禺修建洛溪大桥，让珠江不再是河两岸交流的交通阻碍。

霍英东在南沙倾注了巨额资金和大量心血。他生前曾多次说过，自己有一个“南沙梦”，希望将南沙建设成广东乃至全国对外开放的窗口。

1992年，霍英东买下南沙滨海地区22平方公里土地进行运作开发。2002年起，先后修建了南沙大酒店、世贸中心大厦等标志性建筑及东发码头、南沙客运港、虎门渡轮码头、南沙资讯科技园区等。据说，霍英东25年在南沙投资60亿。这笔钱可以买下两个广州地标建筑“小蛮腰”（一个形状婀娜、400多米高的电视塔），或者在内地城市打造一个占地近100万平方米的旅游观光小镇。

在广阔的土地上进行开发，仅靠一个企业，速度即使不能说缓慢，但也很难强行说快。

世界上90%的发达城市都在沿海地区。以世界最强大的美国为例，纽约、波士顿、费城、华盛顿、西雅图、旧金山、洛杉矶、休斯敦、亚特兰大、迈阿密都是沿海地区。日本全国都是狭长的沿海地区。过去，广州的发展一直依赖于珠江两岸，靠水而建，靠水发展。然而，随着城市的发展，广州必须从靠水走向靠海，作为广州唯一靠海的区域，南沙毫无疑问地成为发展的核心。

一切都是好的！南沙和霍家一起，在等待着一个新的契机，现在看来，也许这个契机应该叫“自贸区”。

2014年12月，国务院决定设立中国（广东）自由贸易试验区，广东自贸区涵盖三片区：广州南沙新区片区（广州南沙自贸区）、深圳前海蛇口片区（深圳前海蛇口自贸区）、珠海横琴新区片区（珠海横琴自贸区），总面积116.2平方公里。

中国自由贸易区是中国深化改革开放的新节点。它是一种多功能经济性特区，在国境内关外设立，以优惠税收和海关特殊监管政策为主要手段，以贸易自由化、便利化为主要目的。2013年9月29日中国（上海）自由贸易试验区正式成立，成为中国第一个自贸区。

中国（广东）自由贸易试验区其实是分布在广州、深圳和珠海三个城市。广州南沙新区片区的面积达到60平方公里（含广州南沙保税港区7.06平方公里）。

在中国（广东）自由贸易试验区广州南沙新区片区的官方网站上，对南沙自贸试验区有着详细的介绍："南沙自贸试验区致力于构建与国际新规则体系相适应的法治化国际化营商环境，率先实现与港澳服务贸易自由化，打造国际贸易功能集成度高、金融创新服务功能强的国际航运物流中心，形成21世纪海上丝绸之路沿线国家和地区科技创新合作的示范基地，建成港澳向内地拓展、内地借助港澳通达国际市场的双向通道和重要平台，为国家构建开放型经济新格局发挥重要作用。"

南沙自贸试验片区挂牌以来，率先推行"一口受理"新模式，"一照一码"改革在全国率先拓展至工商、质监、国税等13个部门，全国首创政府购买查验服务、全国首创海关快速验放机制、全国首创"智检口岸"……

南沙自贸试验片区，创造了为人瞩目的广东"自贸区速度"。

深圳：“后生”城市紧追世界

小渔村的巨变

从一个小渔村发展成一个超级大城市，需要多少年，中国深圳给出的答案是30年。

中国人乐于进行归类和排序，比如四大发明、武林五大高手，城市也是这样。20世纪90年代，人们还习惯将最大的三个城市简称为“京津沪”（北京、天津和上海）。但在这个世纪开始，这一说法逐步过渡到“北上广”（北京、上海和广州），2010年前后，人们更习惯称为“北上广深“，后起之秀深圳在中国的城市格局中已是超级城市，并被广泛接受。

经济特区的拥趸可说出若干成功典范，最成功的莫过于中国香港附近后来被称为“深圳奇迹”的这一个。

由于要考虑可能存在的风险，中国不敢一下子在全国范围实施经济改革，于是设立了深圳特区来做试验，有些出乎意料的是，它吸引了成千上万的外国投资者，在这里经过检验的政策随即被推广到其他城市，包括后来的上海。

1983年，深圳发行中国第一张股票，掀起中国“一夜暴富”的炒股热潮，土地市场首次拍卖，创造出老板、下海、股份公司、外来工、炒鱿鱼、跳槽等新名词和生活方式……过去30多年，深圳创下了难以计数的"中国第一"。

深圳改革的开始，源于紧邻海湾的蛇口响起建设号角。袁庚，深圳特区历史上乃至中国改革开放历程中最为耀眼的名字之一。他当年在蛇口工业区的锐意改革、种种探索，如今看来，仍然具有时代意义。

招商局，把1872年的晚清重臣李鸿章和1978年的共产党员袁庚联系在一起。

1872年，李鸿章上书同治请求设立招商局，奏折呈上三天之后被批准。1978年10月，袁庚以招商局第29代"掌门人"的身份呈报中共中央《关于充分利用香港招商局问题的请示》，请求设立蛇口工业区，也是在三天后获得认可。

1978年，袁庚已是61岁，在中国被称作"过花甲"之年。这个年纪，很多人已安享晚年生活，但袁庚的新事业才刚刚开始。

他把"时间就是金钱、效率就是生命"的牌子立在蛇口的大路上，试验打破干部终身制，他把指名道姓批评自己的文章一字不差地登报。面对莫须有的指责，袁庚艰难却也坚定地在蛇口进行改革，从经济到政治领域，从社会到文化领域。

蛇口的发展变化是深圳改革开放的缩影。

1979年至1988年袁庚主管特区工作十年间，国务院原副总理谷牧先后12次到深圳经济特区检查。特区初期几乎所有的重大决策，都是在他的参与下制定实施的。

负责筹办广东省3个经济特区的吴南生最早提出"广东先走一步"，并以"要杀头就杀我"的豪言，主动请缨办特区。

当然，深圳人最感念的人是邓小平。他为深圳命名"经济特区”。这发生在1984年的1月24日至2月5日，邓小平到广东时视察深圳。

邓小平是中国社会主义改革开放和现代化建设的总设计师。在中国，人们更愿意尊敬而不失亲切地称他为“小平同志”。

2000年11月，邓小平雕像在深圳莲花山顶揭幕，这是中国国内第一座由中央批准、以城市雕塑形式竖立的邓小平雕像。

莲花山顶邓小平铜塑像高6米，重6吨，塑造的小平形象身穿风衣，面朝南方，大步向前，风衣的一角在身后吹起。从莲花山北面上到山顶，迎面首先看到的是影壁，上面刻着邓小平的原话：“深圳的发展和经验证明，我们建立经济特区的政策是正确的。”绕过影壁另一面能看到用隶书写的：“我是中国人民的儿子，我深深地爱着我的祖国和人民。”

1990年前后，国际国内形势发生深刻变化，经济特区和改革开放事业的发展再次面临阻力。在这样的关键时刻，邓小平再次来到广东视察。那是1992年1月19日至1月29日，他在深圳视察四天，在珠海视察七天。这一年的1月18日到2月21日，邓小平先后到武昌、深圳、珠海、上海等地并发表重要谈话，提出“要抓紧有利时机，加快改革开放步伐，力争国民经济更好地上一个新台阶”的要求，为中国走上有中国特色社会主义市场经济发展道路奠定了思想基础。

1月21日，邓小平在国贸大厦发表了视察途中最重要的一次讲话。“要警惕右，但主要是防‘左’。特区发展了十几年才有今天的样子，垮起来是一夜之间哪！……只有经济发展了，人民生活上去了，他们才会相信你，支持你，拥护你。坚持以经济建设为中心的基本路线不是管十年，二十年，是要管一百年！动摇不得。只要我们不坚持社会主义，不改革开放，不发展经济，不改善人民生活，走任何一条路，都是死路！"

国贸大厦被称为"深圳经济特区的窗口"，也是"中国改革开放的象征"。

1984年，高160米、共53层的国贸大厦仅14个月便宣告竣工，创造了"3天一层楼"的奇迹。主楼开建后，先是7天建一层，后来速度提升到5天、4天一层。从第30层开始，持续以3天盖一层的速度。因国贸大厦而开始流传的"深圳速度"，已经成为一个高速度高效益的新概念，成为改革开放后中国建设发展的象征。

移民之城

30多年的时间，深圳从一个仅有3万多人口、两三条小街的边陲小镇，发展成为一座拥有上千万人口，经济繁荣、社会和谐、功能完备、环境优美的现代化都市，创造了世界工业化、城市化、现代化史上的奇迹。

在深圳的发展历程中，更多不知名的人无疑为这个城市的建设也在做着特别的贡献，这些贡献看似微不足道，但却实实在在，并成为推动城市前进的巨大合力。正应了中国的那句古诗“润物细无声”，意思是春雨随着春风在夜里悄悄地落下，悄然无声地滋润着大地万物。

深圳是中国最为典型的移民城市。1979年深圳刚刚建市时，下辖人口只有三十几万。到2015年底，其常住人口已经达到1137.89万，成为名副其实的移民之城，也是中国最大的移民之城。

1982年7月，2万基建工程兵从上海、天津、唐山等地集结南下，集体转业为建筑工人，20世纪80年代深圳1/4的高楼都出自基建工程兵之手。

某种意义上，深圳30年的历史就是一部深圳移民的奋斗史。他们从全国各地携带梦想而来，从无到有，和这座城市一起经历奋斗、繁荣、迷茫与转型，一起享受成功，再一起迎接新挑战。

对这些人的褒奖在2009年达到一个特别的高潮。这一年，美国《时代》周刊评选2009年年度人物，其中就包括"中国工人"。

"中国工人"作为榜单上的唯一一个群体，排在仅次于美联储主席的第二位。《时代》周刊点评说："中国有这么一个词：'保8'，意思是保持每年8%的经济增长率，中国政府认为这对确保社会稳定至关重要。尽管一年前许多人认为这是一个梦想，但是中国做到了，在世界主要经济体中继续保持最快的发展速度，并带领世界走向经济复苏，这些功劳首先要归功于中国千千万万勤劳坚韧的普通工人。"

不管是在历史还是在当下，中国工人都是一支伟大的、出色的、贡献卓著的队伍。新中国成立以来，尤其是改革开放30多年来，千千万万中国工人，用他们辛勤劳动与卓越奉献，成为推动中国经济发展和社会全面进步的最重要力量之一。

创新之都

2015年，华为累计申请了52550件国内专利和30613件外国专利，专利申请总量位居全球第一。2015年，华为以3898件专利申请量蝉联全球企业专利排名榜首。

不过，申请数量并不意味着一家企业在专利上面的积累和优势，被授权的专利才可以拥有真正话语权！也就是在2015年，苹果向华为许可专利98件，而华为向苹果许可专利769件。

华为手机在中国市场后起直追，直追苹果和三星，靠的是过硬的品质。

1987年注册成立的华为技术有限公司，是一家生产销售通信设备的民营通信科技公司，2016年底，他有17万多名员工，华为的产品和解决方案已经应用于全球170多个国家，服务全球运营商50强中的45家及全球1/3的人口。从服务国家和人口来说，华为是一个全球化的公司，但它的总部在深圳。它就是一家在深圳发展起来的公司。

华为成为深圳创新的象征，也是深圳这个城市创新发展的展示。深圳因创新而生，已成为中国人心目中的“创客之都”“创新之城”。除了华为，深圳还有中兴、腾讯、大疆以及华大基因等知名公司。

1998年成立的腾讯公司，是中国最大的互联网综合服务提供商之一，也是中国服务用户最多的互联网企业之一。腾讯最为中国人熟知的产品是QQ和微信，在某种程度上，这两款产品名称已有着自身的含义，就像中国人提到苹果不会以为它仅仅只是一种水果，还应是一家美国公司以及它生产的产品。

腾讯公司董事会主席马化腾13岁来到深圳，1998年带着5个人的团队和50万元的资金研发出了QQ软件。资金和技术一度成为腾讯发展的瓶颈，让马化腾夜不能寐。最困难的时候，他几度想卖掉QQ。但他坚持下来的结果是，2015年6月，腾讯市值在全球互联网公司中排名第五，2014年年收入789亿元。

在前沿科技领域创新创业的大疆创新科技有限公司与华大基因同样被视为深圳创新典范。大疆创新被称作是无人机界的神级公司，占据全球无人机半数以上的市场份额，它的产品已被用于航拍、电影、农业、新闻、能源、遥感测绘等众多领域，并不断地融入新的行业应用。华大基因则通过基因科技造福人类，这家成立于1999年的公司，是全球最大的基因组学研发机构。它以“产学研”一体化的创新发展模式引领基因组学的发展，通过遍布全球的分支机构与产业链各方建立广泛的合作，将前沿的多组学科研成果应用于医学健康、农业育种、资源保存等领域，推动基因科技成果转化，实现基因科技造福人类。华大基因入选2015年全球成长型公司。一般来说，全球成长型公司被视为市场的开拓者、创新者与塑造者。

如果说深圳仅仅是由这些明星公司来代言城市的创新能力，是不全面的。“自主创新”已成为这座城市发展的主导战略。深圳全社会研发投入逐年提升，2015年占GDP比重已升至4.05%，相当于全国平均水平的两倍。PCT（专利合作条约）国际专利申请量和每万人发明专利拥有量居中国各大中城市首位，4G技术、基因测序、超材料、3D显示等领域创新能力跻身世界前沿。

2014年，深圳PCT国际专利申请量达到1.16万件，同比增长15.9%，连续11年居全国各大中城市之首；每万人发明专利拥有量达到66.7件，居全国各大中城市首位。在福布斯发布的“中美创新人物”名单中，中国有10人，深圳占5席。在2014年中国科学十大进展中，深圳两项研究成果入选。企业成为深圳的市场主体，成为创新主体。

作为全球创新链上最为独特的创新之城、中国一线城市中最年轻的城市，深圳一直不断探寻新的经济增长动力，发展为最适合全球创客的舞台。

山寨远去，智慧归来

经过改革开放30多年的积累，深圳已拥有较为完善的上下游产业链，形成了硬件领域科技、资本、信息、人才的聚集。国内最大的开源硬件制造商——矽递科技创始人潘昊谈及来深圳创业的初衷时说，自己在华强北转了一天，就被这里完美的硬件配套所折服。国际知名机构、硬件孵化中心HAXLR8R的创始人Cyril Eberswei1er把总部从硅谷搬到了深圳，他说："这里能够让我们在1公里之内找到任何想要的原材料，这是美国、欧洲和世界上任何地方都做不到的，因为那里没有深圳的华强北。"另一名落户深圳的印度创客也表示，不管多复杂的设计，在这里不到一周的时间就能生产出样品来。

在深圳，华强北周边不超过一公里的范围内，就能找到创客想要的所有原材料，不到一周的时间，就能完成"产品原型—产品—小批量生产"的整个过程，而成本可能只相当于硅谷的1%到5%。一名中关村早期创业者问儿子："为什么一定要大老远跑到深圳办公司？"儿子回答说，找一块IC，在深圳两个星期就够了，但在别的地方可能要两个月；做一块PCB板，深圳及周边地区加工厂多，质量好又便宜。这就是深圳的制造业基础加上市场经济高度发育积累起来的产业链优势。这种优势让创新在深圳变成更便捷，让深圳变成了“创客天堂”。

华强北，日均人流量曾达到约50万人次，年交易额超3000亿元，是全国规模最大、科技含量最高、产品种类最齐全、年交易额最大的电子产品交易集散地，一度被视为中国电子行业的“风向标”和“晴雨表”。这里的电子元器件交易量占深圳市电子通讯市场总数的95%。

不过，巨大的交易下，各种仿造的电子产品也不断出现。一款苹果手机上市，一个月后也许在华强北花几百块钱就能买到一个外形极其相似的手机，只是商标从苹果换成被咬了一口的橘子。它们用低廉的价格与极快的出新速度，将那些既需要内部检测又需要入网检测的国产手机品牌打得落花流水。

也正因此，华强北一度被视为“山寨”的代名词，被最大的“山寨”手机生产地之名所累。

“山寨”本义指山中的城寨，更多的是被指为模仿、复制、抄袭而来的产品。

如果说山寨手机还能赚取利润，在山寨平板电脑时代，200块左右的平板电脑到处都是。山寨厂家们用白菜价迅速在深圳扎根成长，再被白菜价逼得关门歇业，退出市场。

山寨和创新其实是硬币的两面。“当大多人忽视了类似华强北中小企业的时候，更多人觉得这些企业只会山寨，我们相信他们是产业变革的力量。”阿里巴巴技术委员会主席王坚在《在线》一书中这样认为。

Fab Lab创始人尼尔·哥申菲尔德就认为山寨也是非常好的创新

方式。他说，自己喜欢华强北，给儿子买了一个像AppleWatch的产品，比AppleWatch更好，里面还有手机功能。做这种手表，要有这样那样的功能，这也是先进性的技术。在Fab2.0里，我们也可以做一些个性化制造，对所有的功能进行设计、建模、分装等，去研究怎样复制这个功能，而不是做一个假的AppleWatch。"我们所说的复制，是指你有能力超越产品现在的功能范围。"

2010年底，深圳开始组织打击侵犯知识产权和制售假冒伪劣商品的专项行动，持续了半年以上，最终导致3600余商户退出华强北电子市场，进行了一次大规模的手机行业洗牌。

此外，由于深圳地铁7号线施工，自2013年3月起，华强北主干道进行了围挡，改造提升，华强北一度出现空铺现象严重、租金持续下滑的现象。

2016年底，华强北重新开街，并首次以"步行街"身份崭新亮相。过去30年，华强北成长为"中国电子第一街"。未来五到十年，华强北将致力于成为"全国最具影响力、辐射海内外的高端电子信息服务、展示和交易中心、多元业态混合的高品质商业中心和生产型服务业中心，兼有商务办公、居住等功能的城市综合性片区"。

深圳对创新有着清晰的认识，要建立一个综合创新生态体系，通过创新链把各种创新要素形成一个正向的振荡，就是科研资金最早投入，最后通过成果，通过金融创新走下来，走到最后再回到科研创新进行新一轮的更高技术、更高水平的创新，形成一个正向的振荡。

佛山：佛光普照的城市

把中国菜“炒”到全世界

顺德，与东莞、中山、南海并称“广东四小虎”，“2014中国百强区第一名”。在中国的基本话语体系中，进入排行榜单的前列，说明这个城市的与众不同。

顺德意为“顺天明德”，这是广东佛山市的一个区，它自古经济发达，商业繁荣，文教鼎盛。

2014年12月，联合国教科文组织向顺德颁发了“世界美食之都”牌匾，顺德正式成为联合国教科文组织全球创意城市网络组织的成员。

当时，全球有6座城市被联合国教科文组织授予的“美食之都”，分别是哥伦比亚的波帕扬、中国成都、瑞典的厄·特松德、黎巴嫩扎赫勒、韩国全州、中国佛山的顺德。

联合国教科文组织驻京办主任辛格说：“顺德作为粤菜中的代表，有非常优越的特色，而且在世界各地都有顺德的餐馆，这个是顺德美食能推向全世界的一个很重要的地方。今后，我们也将会提供一个更国际化的平台协助顺德美食推广到全世界。”

美食，成为顺德——这个面积不到1000平方公里的城市——最重要的标签之一。中国人对美食文化情有独钟，所以古代的谚语即有“民以食为天”。

粤菜即广东菜，是中国传统四大菜系之一。狭义上的粤菜指广州府菜，包括顺(德)、南(海)、番(禺)。

粤菜因其选料严格、做工精细、中西结合、质鲜味美、养生保健等特点而名扬天下。作为在海外影响力最大的中国菜系，粤菜馆遍布全球，因此有“有华人的地方就有粤菜”的说法。

顺德是粤菜最重要的发源地之一，它是佛山的五个区之一，顺德的美食文化也是佛山的缩影。据不完全统计，佛山市登记在册的厨点师就有近千人，其中很多是国家级特级烹饪大师。

2014年的统计数据显示，顺德有“中国烹饪大师”9位、“中国烹饪名师”34位、“中华餐饮名店”21家、“中华名小吃”11种，是国内烹饪大师、餐饮名店最密集的地区之一。2004年，被中国烹饪协会评为“中国厨师之乡”；2010年又获评“中华美食名城”。顺德平均每17个人当中就有一个人从事餐饮行业。

一个世纪以来，佛山餐饮业群星闪耀，涌现了众多的著名厨师。上世纪20—30年代，谭杰南在广州开办的陶陶居、七妙斋和大同酒家，至今仍享有盛名。

“陶陶居”寓意来此品茗乐也陶陶。陶陶居是广州最有名气的茶楼之一，主要经营名茶、茶点、茶食及酒菜餐饮。广东人喜欢饮茶，尤其喜欢去茶馆喝早茶，茶客坐定，服务员前来请茶客点茶和糕点，早茶也成为广州的独特城市文化。

上世纪30—50年代佛山名厨有崔强、黎和、王瑞、陆贞，被誉为广东饮食业的四大天王；50—60年代有罗坤、潘同。

尤为难得的是，顺德两位国厨萧良初、康辉为主厨的团队，先后开创了上海、北京之南北国宴。萧良初从1951年作为首任总厨任职新中国第一个国宾馆——上海锦江饭店，先后为100多个国家的国王、总统、首相、总理等政要主厨或安排菜式。

1954年周恩来总理参加日内瓦会议，萧良初是随行厨师。其间周总理请喜剧大师卓别林吃饭，主宾谈兴甚欢，卓别林吃完意犹未尽，专门请萧良初加做了一道香酥鸡，打包回家与家人分享。

1961年，周恩来总理率领中国代表团出席日内瓦扩大会议。萧良初被点名随团掌勺，其拿手菜八珍盐焗鸡等佳肴得到各国贵宾赞赏。

康辉曾任北京饭店行政总厨，并负责筹建钓鱼台国宾馆和人民大会堂餐厅。2002年，他成为被授予国宝级的中国12位“中国烹饪大师”之一。

中国功夫“漂洋”去

1999年《时代周刊》列出20世纪英雄与偶像人物名单，在这份榜单中，有英国已故黛安娜王妃、拳王阿里、玛丽莲·梦露、美国总统肯尼迪、球王贝利。但对中国人来说，最为熟悉的应该是这位黄皮肤、拍照时经常一脸桀骜不驯的功夫巨星李小龙，他就是中国功夫的代言人，就像迈克尔·乔丹是篮球的标志、贝利是现代足球的标志。

2000年，美国政府宣布发行一套《李小龙诞辰60周年纪念邮票》，这是继玛丽莲·梦露和007后第三位获此殊荣的艺人，也是华人第一人。2003年美国《黑带》杂志推出李小龙逝世30周年纪念专辑，表明“李小龙对美国武术界的恒久影响”。

Kung fu，英语中这样称呼中国功夫，这本是佛山和珠江三角洲中部地区对武术的俗称。在语言翻译中，直接音译或者是因为它难以翻译，或者是因为它很重要，功夫显然应属后者。让世界迷上中国功夫的人无疑就是李小龙。

李小龙的祖籍就在广东顺德均安镇，顺德所在的佛山市，是中国的功夫之乡。全球最大的李小龙纪念馆就在均安镇，这个总用地面积达到3.7万平方米的大型展馆在2008年开始对外开放。

佛山是中国南派功夫的主要发源地。2004年，佛山被授予中国“武术之城”称号。明初，佛山功夫已相当普及。清末民初，佛山功夫流派纷呈，涌现出一批有国际影响的武术名家和武术组织，并通过各种途径走向世界，世界上广泛流行的蔡李佛拳、洪拳、咏春拳等不少拳种和流派其根都在佛山，著名武术大师黄飞鸿、咏春宗师梁赞、叶问祖籍及师承亦在佛山。

李小龙为太多人所熟知。他是世界武道变革先驱者、武术技击家、武术哲学家、UFC开创者、MMA之父、武术宗师、功夫片的开创者和截拳道创始人、华人武打电影演员、中国功夫首位全球推广者、好莱坞首位华人演员。他在香港的四部半电影3次打破多项纪录，其中《猛龙过江》打破了亚洲电影票房纪录，与好莱坞合作的《龙争虎斗》全球总票房达2.3亿美元。美国报刊甚至把李小龙誉为“功夫之王”，日本人称他为“武之圣者”，香港报纸也赞誉他为“当代中国武术及电影史上的奇才”。

正是在李小龙之后，中国多位功夫明星走上世界舞台。其中就包括成龙和李连杰。

与李小龙直接展示功夫的刚硬不同，成龙将武术与戏曲杂耍嫁接，在注重动作的观赏性同时，减少了功夫电影中常见的血腥暴力场面，开创了功夫喜剧的先河。

回首当年，李小龙出生在美国，但他的童年和少年时光是在香港度过。小时候的李小龙身体十分瘦弱，父亲为了强壮儿子的体魄，便教其打太极拳。李小龙自己本就喜欢尝试新事物，酷爱冒险，特别是户外运动。于是他迷上了武术，除了太极拳，他还学过咏春拳、洪拳、少林拳等拳种，为今后自创打下了基础。

1967年，李小龙在美国创立了跨越门派限制的、世界性的现代中国功夫“科学的街头格斗技”——截拳道（Jeet Kune Do），那年他27岁。这是一种融合世界各种武术精华的全方位自由搏击术。但很多人认为，截拳道中有咏春拳的影子。毫无疑问，这来自于他的师傅叶问。

1893年出生的叶问，祖籍广东省南海县桑园，上世纪50年代开始在香港教授咏春拳。其封门弟子梁挺将咏春拳传扬国际，更通过其子弟在全球广泛传扬，形成出一套最权威的中国传统武术实战修习课程《梁挺咏春》（WingTsun），载誉全球。叶问1972年去世后，其子叶准、叶正致力于向海外推广咏春拳术，叶准还曾获得美国奥委会的嘉奖。

另外一位中国功夫明星李连杰生于北京，他创纪录地在1975年至1979年间连续五年获得中国武术全能冠军。如果不是在1982年主演电影《少林寺》，他可能只是一个优秀的武术队员而不是武打明星。

《少林寺》引起的轰动，可以用下面的事实说明：这部内地以当时一角钱的票价，累计票房达1亿元人民币。也就是说，他的电影曾被至少观看10亿次。

李连杰拍摄的最为经典的电影就是《黄飞鸿》系列。90年初，李连杰接受邀请出演《黄飞鸿之壮志凌云》，在香港引起轰动，之后他一连拍了五部《黄飞鸿》系列电影。在中国，以黄飞鸿为主题拍摄的电影多达上百部，创造世界之最。

当然，电影中的黄飞鸿并非与现实完全相符。黄飞鸿1856年出生于佛山市南海县，他是清末民初的洪拳大师，岭南武术界一代宗师。在南派武术的发展中有着重要的影响，他的一生充满传奇色彩，曾追随著名爱国将领刘永福在抗日保台战争中立下功勋。他还是位济世为怀、救死扶伤名医。他还善于舞狮，有广州狮王之称。

佛山梦想

美食和功夫让佛山誉满天下，成为文化名城和广府文化的核心地带。但被誉为全国先进制造业基地、广东重要的制造业中心，对佛山来说，也同样重要。

佛山“肇迹于晋，得名于唐”。500年前，中国正值明朝中后期，在这个传统农业大国之内，生产分工更加细化，出现了脱离农业耕作的手工业阶层。那时的中国，出现了商品经济的萌芽，有四个地方尤为突出，被称为“中国四大名镇”。它们是：湖北汉口镇，江西景德镇，河南朱仙镇，以及我们熟悉的广东佛山镇。

我们要讲述的城市——佛山，这个500年前登上中国历史舞台的名镇，正是利用这一时期，迅速崛起成为华南的经济、商贸和文化中心。

明清时期，佛山逐步发展成岭南地区商品集散地和冶铸、陶瓷、纺织、中成药等四大制造业中心。

石湾位于佛山禅城区东南部，这里的陶瓷早就成为佛山亮丽的“名片”，“石湾瓦，甲天下，旁及海外之国”。明、清两代，方圆几公里的石湾小镇就有陶瓷107座，从业人数达6万多人。因为石湾陶瓷，佛山才有了“南国陶都”的声誉。“都”在中国的话语体系中，有一个含义是“头目，首领”，意思是最好的。改革开放后，石湾陶瓷范围更广，品种更多样，规模也更庞大。

更为不可思议的是，佛山不是药材产地，不是棉花产地，没有铁矿，也没有陶泥，但却成就了四大制造业中心。有人形象地称其为“无中生有”。

事实上，佛山手工业的兴盛，与外来人口的南迁离不开关系。南宋后期，中原人口为避战事南迁，手工业者随之南迁。到明清时期，佛山手工业发展到达巅峰，遍布全镇有620多条大小街巷，60多处渡口，镇内形成了专业街市有二十八铺，各行各业兴旺发达。

1872年，36岁的广东南海西樵简村人陈启沅从南洋返回家乡。第二年，他用自己设计的机器，创办了我国一家民族资本缫丝业企业。25岁时，他就随兄长到越南经商致富，或许是为了对“继续昌盛兴隆”的美好期待，厂子取名“继昌隆”。

继昌隆缫丝厂规模很大，由于经营得法，生意畅旺，产品远销海内外，收益颇丰。为了荣耀乡梓，他大兴土林，在简村建造了当时极具豪华的“百业坊”住宅群，成为名扬天下的大富商。

继昌隆缫丝厂是中国第一家民族资本经营的机器缫丝厂，它的成立标志着缫丝工业进入了新的历史时期，促进了珠江三角洲乃至全国缫丝工业的发展。

佛山还诞生了中国第一家火柴厂——巧明火柴厂，那是清光绪五年(1879年)，创始人卫省轩青年时目睹火柴从国外输入，令财源外流。于是，他到日本学习火柴生产技术，回国后在佛山文昌沙创办巧明火柴厂。

以中国第一家新式缫丝厂和第一家火柴厂作为标志，引领风气之先的佛山成为中国近代民族工业的发源地之一。

如今，佛山成为珠三角经济区重要的商贸中心之一，全国流通领域物流示范城市，拥有一批投资规模大、辐射能力强的物流交易配送中心。佛山是中国六个品牌之都之一、国家商标战略实施示范城市、中国品牌经济城市。以制造业发达著称的佛山市，工业发展历史源远流长，尤其是传统制造业优势明显，拥有包括“美的”“海天”等一批具有较好工业旅游要素的知名企业。以石湾陶艺为代表的陶瓷制造业，集聚了上百家各类工业用瓷砖及卫浴产品；以香云纱、彩灯、玉器等为代表的历史悠久艺术产业，成为人文历史类的完美代表；以海天酱油、顺德制糖为代表的食品工业，见证了岭南食品产业的历史发展过程。

东莞：制造业名城艰难爬坡

两城之间的奇迹

东莞，位于珠江口东岸。珠江，中国第三大河，在广东流入大海，包括东莞在内的多个城市受其滋养，被称为珠江三角洲，这是中国经济最发达的地区之一。特别是，东莞是在广州、深圳两个大城市的中间，距离广州和深圳中心城区均不到一小时的车程，却奇迹般地创造了完全不同于这两者的生长之路，保持着自己的精神特色。

曾有外国专家说“10多年前从卫星地图上看，广州和深圳之间还是一片空白，几年间在这片空白处冒出了一座城市。”不得不说，这是中国城建史和经济史上的奇迹。

东莞是中国城市乃至中国发展的缩影，快得让人目瞪口呆。莞城是东莞的一个镇，镇在中国是县和县级市以下的行政区划单位。通常地级市下设县，县下设镇。但东莞成为“特殊的一个”，是中国为数不多的不设区、县的地级市，被俗称为“直筒子”市。

莞城只是东莞30多个街道和镇中的一个，但它一直以来都是东莞市的政治、经济和文化中心，具有悠久的历史和深厚的文化底蕴。

在中国，文化底蕴主要体现在一个城市的历史中。广东清代四大名园之一、全国重点文物保护单位可园坐落在这座千年古城。可园的意思就是这个庭园“可堪游赏”。可园又是当时文人雅集地。作为全国重点文物单位，可园在近代广东艺术史和建筑史上都占有重要地位。

中国人习惯讲唐诗宋词，苏轼在文、诗、词三方面都达到了极高的造诣，堪称宋代文学最高成就的代表。他与东莞的资福寺就有不为人知的渊源，他不仅曾夜宿资福寺，还于公元1100年写下三篇文章，名为《广州东莞县资福禅寺罗汉阁记》《广州东莞县资福寺舍利塔铭》《广州东莞资福堂老柏再生赞》，流传至今。

在百度搜索中输入“莞城”二字，最先呈现的搜索结果里有名为“文化莞城”的网页，可见文化在莞城中的独特地位以及给这座城市留下的痕迹，其实这是莞城街道办的官方网站。百度可以简单理解成中国的google，在中文的网络搜索世界里最为知名，它的名字据说来源于中国知名的一句诗词：众里寻他千百度，蓦然回首，那人却在灯火阑珊处。这是宋朝时又一位著名的词人辛弃疾的代表作品，这句话的意思是“我在人群中寻找她千百回，猛然一回头，不经意间却在灯火零落之处发现了她”。寻她千百回，正是网络搜索的真实写照。

网站对莞城做了这样的介绍：东莞市莞城街道有1700多年的悠久历史，从唐至德二年（757年）以来，一直是东莞（县）市治的所在地。文化源远流长，文物古迹众多。

不仅是“虎门销烟”

东莞被中国人熟知更多是因为“虎门销烟”。19世纪80年代，由于鸦片输入的急剧增加，使中英两国的贸易地位完全改变。英国由原来的入超变为出超，中国却相反，造成白银大量外流。据统计，1820—1840年间，中国外流白银在1亿两左右。由鸦片大量输入而引起的白银不断外流，已开始扰乱清王朝的国库和货币的流通，使清朝的经济面临崩溃的边缘。更为严重的是，鸦片的泛滥极大地摧残了吸食者的身心健康，任何一个国家都不可能任其发展。1839年6月，中国的清朝政府委任钦差大臣林则徐在广东虎门集中销毁鸦片。从6月3日到25日，23天的时间销毁鸦片19187箱和2119袋，总重量100多万公斤。虎门，这个东莞临海的小镇，因揭开了中国近代史的这一页，闻名中外。

林则徐一生力抗外敌入侵，因其主张严禁鸦片，在中国有“民族英雄”之誉。但他对于西方的文化、科技和贸易则持开放态度，主张学其优而用之。根据文献记载，他至少略通英、葡两种外语，且着力翻译西方报刊和书籍。晚清思想家魏源将林则徐及幕僚翻译的文书合编为《海国图志》，此书对晚清的洋务运动乃至日本的明治维新都有启发作用。

“虎门销烟”让虎门这个东莞小镇成为中国人心目中尽管没去过但一定听过的地方。不过，一个城市获得尊重不可能仅靠历史上的那些瞬间。东莞在改革开放以来创造出的“东莞奇迹”，被誉为“中国改革开放一个精彩而生动的缩影”，成为中国改革开放的先进典型，才是我们对这个城市不断投射关注更重要的原因。

中国共产党第十一届中央委员会第三次全体会议召开。诺贝尔经济学奖得主、新制度经济学鼻祖罗纳德·哈里·科斯在关于中国市场经济之路的著作《变革中国》中这样评价这次会议：“是共和国历史上意义重大的一次会议，它不仅重新巩固了中国共产党的政权，还为重新凝聚千疮百孔的社会铺平了道路。会议将中国人民的能量、热忱和创造力重新拉回到社会主义现代化建设上。”

在这前后，中国逐步明确实行对内改革、对外开放的政策。

1978年11月，安徽省凤阳县小岗村开始实行“分田到户，自负盈亏”的家庭联产承包责任制，拉开了中国对内改革的大幕。1979年7月，广东、福建两省被正式批准在对外经济活动中实行特殊政策、灵活措施，迈开了改革开放的历史性步伐。

改革开放前，东莞一个完全劳动力的日收入最低只有几分钱。但30年后的2008年，东莞经济年平均增长18%，创造了比亚洲“四小龙”起飞时速度更快、周期更长的高增长奇迹，成为中国经济发展最快的地区之一，综合经济实力位居全国大中城市第十二位。而事实上，东莞的面积与内地不少县城相比，并不大多少甚至更小。

“亚洲四小龙”在英文世界被称为“Four Asian Tigers”(亚洲四虎)。龙是中华民族最具代表性的文化象征之一。亚洲四小龙指的是从20世纪60年代开始，中国香港、新加坡、韩国和中国台湾推行出口导向型战略，重点发展劳动密集型的加工产业，在短时间内实现了经济的腾飞，一跃成为全亚洲发达富裕的地区，曾被认为是亚洲经济崛起的代表。在相当长的时间内，“亚洲四小龙”成为中国尤其是沿海省份的楷模。

1992年，邓小平视察南方时曾提出，广东应争取在20年里赶超“亚洲四小龙”。广东是东莞所在的省份，它的经济总量曾长期是中国经济总量的1/7。如果对标世界上的国家经济，广东与韩国相当，排名世界十几位。

通过广东的发展可以看出东莞发展的脉络。世界银行前首席亚太经济学家卡拉斯曾对“东莞奇迹”惊叹不已："东莞，中国南方的一个城市，它在过去20年一直保持着每年20%的增长速度，在它境内可获得95％制造和组装电脑所需的零部件，它被誉为‘世界工厂’。"

卡拉斯还在他的学术报告《东亚复兴：增长的理念》中谈到，东莞在1978年时只是珠江边一片大大小小的村镇，其人口主要靠捕鱼和耕田为生，但在今天东莞有接近700万的人口，500多万是外来员工，散布在数以千计的工厂，创造出一系列令人眼花缭乱的产品。

东莞模式

东莞的秘诀何在？或者说中国经济快速发展的秘诀何在？答案之一，也可能是最重要的答案：利用外资，走外向型经济发展道路。

1978年7月，国务院（中央人民政府，是中国最高国家权力机关的执行机关，是最高国家行政机关）颁发了《开展对外加工装配业务试行办法》，广东作为中国改革开放的先行地区和前沿阵地，率先作出发展来料加工的决定。东莞利用自己的地缘优势和华侨港澳同胞众多的人缘优势，开始了引进外资。因资金、技术、人才不足，以“三来一补”作为加工贸易的起步。

“三来一补”指的是来料加工、来样加工、来件装配和补偿贸易，是中国内地在改革开放初期尝试性地创立的一种企业贸易形式，“三来一补”企业主要的结构是：由外商提供设备(包括由外商投资建厂房)、原材料、来样，并负责全部产品的外销，由中国企业提供土地、厂房、劳力。中外双方组成一个新的"三来一补"企业。

中国内地第一家“三来一补”企业——太平手袋厂就在

东莞诞生。这家1978年9月15日成立，工商批文号是粤字001号的企业，前身是虎门太平竹器社。

1978年7月，有两三百人的香港信孚手袋制品公司，因不断上涨的成本被逼到濒临倒闭的边缘。老板张子弥带着几个手袋和一些碎布料，来到东莞虎门，找到了一个叫唐志平的年轻人。

26岁的唐志平当时在太平服装厂负责供销业务。张子弥拿出一个黑色女装手袋和一些手袋半成品的裁片，希望太平服装厂照样子尽快仿制。

曾经有中国的媒体这样报道当时的情景：（张子弥）从包里拿出一个黑色的人造革手袋，给在场工人出了一道他们从未做过的题，即在没有任何图纸和说明的情况下，复制这个手袋。于是，从未见过这种手袋的太平服装厂的三个工人，根据香港客人提供的“吝啬”的毛料，熬了一个通宵，终于用缝纫机按版呈现了一个一模一样的手袋。客人很满意，一个月后便与东莞二轻局签订了为期五年的合同（太平服装厂是东莞二轻局下面的一个企业），东莞第一家“三来一补”企业正式揭开了它的面纱。

太平手袋厂位于虎门镇解放路7号，曾经发生“虎门销烟”的这个地方，又在创造着一个中国的第一。当年风光无限的“粤字001号”，在1996年倒闭，但由于它身上无可取代的历史标签，被包括东莞人在内的国人屡屡提及。

东莞利用外资的星星之火迅速被点燃，“三来一补”企业在东莞像雨后春笋般发展起来。

1988年底，东莞“三来一补”企业达2500多家，遍布80％的乡村。1991年，引入外资高达17亿美元。东莞从一个默默无闻的农业小县城，一跃成为一个全国知名的工业化城市。

“三来一补”企业的成功引起了全国的关注，这种发展方式也被全国各地广泛采用，吸引外资发展经济成为全国潮流。沿海地区许多地方派人来考察学习，借鉴东莞的成功做法。一些媒体和经济学者也驻足东莞，将其总结成享誉全国的“东莞模式”。

“不管黑猫白猫，捉到老鼠就是好猫”，被誉为中国改革开放总设计师的邓小平的“白猫黑猫”论，表达了想问题办事情一切要从实际出发，而不是从条条框框出发的观点；一切要从有利于发展社会生产力，增强国家综合国力，提高人民生活水平的实际出发，社会主义是靠干出来的，不是靠讲出来的。“白猫黑猫”论无疑倡导了一种实干精神。同样广为流传的“摸着石头过河”，也是要强调边干边摸索经验。正是因为这样，不同的地方根据基本情况做的发展探索就会被总结概括，成为某种模式。

“东莞模式”一度成为我国实施沿海发展战略的基本模式，它与“苏南模式”“温州模式”齐名，各自代表不同类型的经济发展模式。不无巧合的是，这三种模式恰恰发生在中国经济实力较强的几个省份：“苏南模式”在江苏省，“温州模式”的浙江省，“东莞模式”在广东省。

“苏南模式”指的是苏南的苏州、无锡和常州通过发展乡镇企业实现非农化发展的方式。苏南模式的主要特征是：农民依靠自己的力量发展乡镇企业；乡镇企业的所有制结构以集体经济为主；乡镇政府主导乡镇企业的发展；市场调节为主要手段。

温州人被称为中国的犹太人，是全中国对市场最敏锐的人群之一，他们总能捕捉到许多市场机会，最先发现市场需求。在市场的孕育下，温州人全力发展轻工制造业。一下子家庭作坊遍布全城，温州人的小商品迅速闻名世界。以此为基础的“温州模式”是指浙江省东南部的温州地区以家庭工业和专业化市场的方式发展非农产业，从而形成小商品、大市场的发展格局。小商品是指生产规模、技术含量和运输成本都较低的商品。大市场是指温州人在全国建立的市场网络。

新的发展需求甚至对政府的管理服务也提出了新要求。东莞为适应改革开放、招商引资的需要，率先成立了全国第一个加工贸易服务办公室，对来东莞办企业的实行一条龙服务，各部门集中在一起解决企业和百姓办事难的问题，大大加速了外资进入东莞的速度。

2007年，东莞在只占全国0.03%的土地上，创造了占全国1.3%的生产总值、1.1%的财政收入、4.9%的出口总额，超越了内地一些省份的经济能量，故外界以“富可敌省”来形容东莞的经济能力。

就是在经济发展过程中，似乎是悄无声息地，东莞迅速进行着城市化进程，从农业县到工业大市。1990年前后，当时东莞农村到处出现了“村村点火、户户冒烟”的繁荣景象。有人将其概括为“城乡一体化的农村城市化道路”。

2016年中国城镇化率达到57.35%。有数据预测，2020年，中国的城市化率将达到60%。而在1978年，这一数字仅仅是17.9%。城市化是人类进步必然要经过的过程，经过了城市化，标志着现代化目标的实现。

1984年，全国农村的改革和发展还处于完善家庭联产承包责任制的阶段，东莞已经完成了农村经济管理体制，开始向商品农业转变，而且由于乡镇企业的快速发展，加速了劳动力向非农产业的转移。于是，当年，东莞提出了“向农村工业化进军”的奋斗目标。

农村工业化推动了城乡一体化和城市化进程。1992年，东莞确立“按现代化城市格局建设东莞”的发展战略，使东莞很快就从原来的农村乡镇变为城乡一体化的组团城市。从2001年开始，东莞掀起新一轮城市建设高潮。

就像中国很多发展中的城市一样，城市与农村的视觉界限已不再那么清晰，农村盖起太多的小洋楼。最近几年，城市人到农村旅游居住似乎变得流行起来，而在30年前，他们想离开的恰恰也是农村。

受益于经济快速发展，东莞在广东率先实行免征农业税、普及高中阶段教育、免除城乡义务教育阶段学生学杂费和书本费，在全国率先实行农（居）民养老保险、农（居）民基本医疗保险和计划生育养老保险制度。

有人认为，这条路子，代表了中国农村走向城市化、实现现代化的方向。中共中央办公厅调研室曾指出“东莞之路提供了我国城市化的一种现实可行的模式”，“对我国实现现代化会得到一些重要启示”。

“东莞塞车，全球缺货”

事情总是在不断变化中，有些向好的方向发展。

即使在上世纪80年代取得惊人的发展成绩，但东莞人没有躺在功劳簿上，而是不断寻找新机会。那时候东莞基本上是劳动密集型产业，技术含量低，附加值低，主要依靠增加外地劳动力来支撑经济增长，经济发展形式粗放。

随着越来越多的IT企业的不断进入，并成群落。东莞经济发生了深刻的变革。东莞的外贸出口总额从1978年的0.39亿美元，增加到2007年的602.32亿美元，增长1543.4倍，年均增长27.7%。东莞成为继深圳、上海之后全国出口额最高的城市，在各地级市中排名第一。

“东莞塞车，全球缺货”，还曾有人这样说“东莞塞车，世界感冒”，因为这里的电脑主板、磁头、驱动器的产量，占了全球的75%以上。“不论你在哪里下单，都在东莞制造”。东莞成为现代制造业名城已是事实。

东莞需要也必须实现产业结构的转型升级，向更高级的经济发展方式转变。1994年东莞对外宣布，东莞已基本实现了农村工业化，这是东莞“第一次工业革命”的结束，接下来要不失时机地推进“第二次工业革命”。

“第二次工业革命”被赋予的内涵是由劳动密集型工业向技术密集型工业迈进，使“数量型”经济逐步向“质量型”经济转变。其被提出和实施，标志着东莞经济开始了升级转型。

东莞抓住了难得的机遇，承接到了第二波的国际产业转移。那时东莞的先进IT产业迅猛发展，东莞被人称为“中国的IT之都”，并办起了电博会，成为当时全球的四大国际电脑资讯博览会之一。东莞是全球最大的电脑零部件生产制造基地，电脑95%的零配件在东莞都有生产。

30多年的时间里，从“三来一补”方式起步，东莞外向型经济产业层次不断提升，产品内涵不断升级，进入80年代主要承接香港纺织、制鞋箱包、玩具等传统制造业，企业规模小，产品附加值低；进入90年代，台湾及日韩地区电脑周边产品为主的IT制造业大量进入东莞，令东莞成为制造之都。

当然不仅仅是IT制造业。东莞最后形成了门类齐全、配套完善、技术先进、涉及30多个行业和6万多种产品的制造业体系，世界上大多数工业产品都可以在东莞企业群体的“工业生物链”中找到其配套的行业和产品。在某种意义上，东莞是“MADE IN CHINA”的样本区域，但凡任何有关制造业的风吹草动，总能在东莞找到分析样本。东莞成了电子信息、电气机械及设备、纺织服装鞋帽、食品饮料、造纸及纸制品等各类制造业的“代工厂”。

东莞还是“鞋业之都”“服装之都”和“玩具之都”。全球每十双鞋中就有一双属于“东莞制造”。它还是“服装之都”，在几乎没有季节交替感觉、12月仍可以穿短袖衣、一根羊毛也不生产的东莞市大朗镇，年销售毛衣超过10亿件，全球平均每5个人就有1人身着大朗生产的毛衣。

江门：
依旧海之门

“侨乡”人杰地灵

我们吃过晚饭，热气已经退了。太阳落下了山坡，只留下一段灿烂的红霞在天边。

我们走过一段石子路，很快就到了河边。在河边大树下，我们发现了几只小船。

我们陆续跳上一只船。一个朋友解开了绳，拿起竹竿一拨，船缓缓地动了，向河中心移去。

河面很宽，白茫茫的水上没有一点波浪。船平静地在水面移动。三支桨有规律地在水里划，那声音就像一支乐曲。

在一个地方，河面变窄了。一簇簇树叶伸到水面上。树叶真绿得可爱。那是许多株茂盛的榕树，看不出主干在什么地方。

当我说许多株榕树的时候，朋友们马上纠正我的错误。一个朋友说那里只有一株榕树，另一个朋友说是两株。我见过不少榕树，这样大的还是第一次看见。

我们的船渐渐逼近榕树了。我有机会看清它的真面目，真是一株大树，枝干的数目不可计数。枝上又生根，有许多根直垂到地上，伸进泥土里。一部分树枝垂到水面，从远处看，就像一株大树卧在水面上。

榕树正在茂盛的时期，好像把它的全部生命力展示给我们看。那么多的绿叶，一簇堆在另一簇上面，不留一点儿缝隙。那翠绿的颜色，明亮地照耀着我们的眼睛，似乎每一片绿叶上都有一个新的生命在颤动。这美丽的南国的树！

船在树下泊了片刻。岸上很湿，我们没有上去。朋友说这里是“鸟的天堂”，有许多鸟在这树上做巢，农民不许人去捉它们。我仿佛听见几只鸟扑翅的声音，等我注意去看，却不见一只鸟的影儿。只有无数的树根立在地上，像许多根木桩。土地是湿的，大概涨潮的时候河水会冲上岸去。“鸟的天堂”里没有一只鸟，我不禁这样想。于是船开了，一个朋友拨着桨，船缓缓地移向河中心。

第二天，我们划着船到一个朋友的家乡去。那是个有山有塔的地方。从学校出发，我们又经过那“鸟的天堂”。

这一次是在早晨。阳光照耀在水面，在树梢，一切都显得更加光明了。我们又把船在树下泊了片刻。

起初周围是静寂的。后来忽然起了一声鸟叫。我们把手一拍，便看见一只大鸟飞了起来。接着又看见第二只，第三只。我们继续拍掌，树上就变得热闹了，到处都是鸟声，到处都是鸟影。大的，小的，花的，黑的，有的站在树枝上叫，有的飞起来，有的在扑翅膀。

我注意地看着，眼睛应接不暇，看清楚了这只，又错过了那只，看见了那只，另一只又飞起来了。一只画眉鸟飞了出来，被我们的掌声一吓，又飞进了叶丛，站在一根小枝上兴奋地叫着，那歌声真好听。

当小船向着高塔下面的乡村划去的时候，我回头看那被抛在后面的茂盛的榕树。我感到一点儿留恋。昨天是我的眼睛骗了我，那“鸟的天堂”的确是鸟的天堂啊！

——巴金《鸟的天堂》

1933年，中国近代最知名的作家之一巴金来到江门市新会区会城镇天马河的河心沙洲游览。岛上有一株500多年历史的大榕树，这棵树的树枝深垂到地上，扎入土中，成为新的树干，随着时间的推移，这棵大榕树竟独木成林，林中栖息着成千上万只鸟雀，巴金有感而发，写出了多次进入小学语文教材的散文——《鸟的天堂》，成为几代中国人的精神记忆。

49年后的1982年，巴金又为这一景观亲笔题名“小鸟天堂”，自此，小鸟天堂名播天下。如今，这里已经是全国最大的天然赏鸟乐园，亦是新会著名的国际级生态旅游景点。

鸟的天堂，就像是江门这座城市特点的写照，鸟儿忽来忽去，但终不会离沙洲而去。人亦如是。

江门地处西江与其支流蓬江汇合处，蓬江北面的蓬莱山与江南的烟墩山对峙似门，故名“江门”。

江门自古是人才辈出之地。“一门三院士，九子皆才俊”，出生于江门新会的近代著名思想家梁启超九个子女，人人成才、各有所长。

梁启超被公认是清末优秀的学者，中国历史上一位百科全书式人物。在结束清王朝统治的辛亥革命前，他与革命派论战中发明了一种新文体，介于古文与白话文之间，平易畅达、句法灵活，深受时人喜爱。梁启超是中国第一个在文章中使用“中华民族”一词的人。

他最为中国人所知的，还是在1895年与数千名举人联名上书清朝的光绪皇帝，反对在甲午战争中失败后签订丧权辱国的《马关条约》，是谓“公车上书”。随后，他与自己的老师康有为在皇帝的支持下发动戊戌变法，提倡科学文化，改革政治、教育制度，发展农、工、商业。

100多天后，变法失败，绝大多数新政都被取消。但中国近代第一所国立大学京师大学堂得以保留。1912年，京师大学堂更名为北京大学。北京大学一直是中国最好的大学之一。

江门地处珠江三角洲西部。江门辖下的新会区（市）、开平市、台山市、恩平市、鹤山市，由于五地人文风俗基本一致，故以“五邑”著称，闻名海内外。祖籍江门的华侨、华人和港澳台同胞近400万，分布在全世界五大洲107个国家和地区，在亚洲地区的约占20%，美洲地区的约占70%。

中国最著名的侨乡有四个：江门、泉州、潮汕、梅州。泉州、潮汕、梅州三个侨乡的华侨大部分在东南亚，只有五邑的华侨主要分布在美国、加拿大和澳大利亚。这使得五邑侨乡在保留中国传统文化的同时，还会积极推动中外文化交流，从建筑、饮食、服饰到风俗习惯，随处可见中西交融的痕迹。

司徒美堂就是其中一位代表。

1868年4月3日，他出生在广东开平县赤坎镇一个农民家庭。1880年3月，年仅12岁的司徒美堂从开平步行至香港，搭乘渡轮，只身远渡美国。

1894年，司徒美堂来到波士顿，成立了安良堂，打出了“锄强扶弱，除暴安良”的旗号，很快就成为洪门致公堂旗下的强势团体，最后发展到全美国31个城市都有安良堂，规模浩大，成员达2万多人。1905年，司徒美堂在纽约成立了“安良总堂”，当时的法律顾问是后来的美国总统——富兰克林·罗斯福。

司徒美堂后与孙中山相识，孙中山在美活动期间，为保护孙中山的安全，他全程当贴身保镖兼厨师。1911年4月，广州黄花岗起义失败后，同盟会急需15万美元救急，司徒美堂发动洪门致公堂的兄弟募捐。但他很清楚，这么庞大的数额靠华侨募捐，断难在短时间内凑齐。情急之下，他把在加拿大多伦多、温哥华、维多利亚和金山大厦的4所致公堂大厦典押出去。后来又变卖几座致公堂大楼，筹足了15万美元，支援了武装起义。同年武昌起义后，孙中山由美归国的旅费，也是司徒美堂等人提供。

1932年，“一·二八”淞沪事变爆发，蔡廷锴将军率领十九路军将士英勇抵抗日寇。消息传到美国，司徒美堂马上组织募捐，带着捐款回到祖国慰问将士，他和蔡廷锴也成了莫逆之交。

“侨”是江门的城市“DNA”，是江门区别于其他城市的根本之处。2015年开始，江门正式启动“中国侨都”建设，提出擦亮“中国侨都”的城市名片。江门市还出台实施了侨务强市规划纲要及行动方案。2016年底，江门市提出，要大力发展全域旅游、建设旅游强市，创建中国国际特色旅游目的地，开平市、台山市被确定为国家全域旅游示范区创建单位。

发展侨务旅游，中国侨都千里“潮人径”成为重要抓手。“潮人径”提倡用脚步去丈量城市的繁华，利用现有公路、村道、林道、登山小道、田园小路等线路，串联自然保护区、风景名胜区、历史古迹、古村落、田园风光等景观节点，形成具有侨乡特色的城乡慢行步行径系统。2017年，江门全市将建设总长达3000公里的“潮人径”。在一段时间内，“潮人径”最后争取达到10000公里，打造“广东第一步行径”。

百年碉楼和侨村

开平赤坎镇一位姓关的老人有30多位亲戚在美国和加拿大生活。在侨乡开平，像他这样的家庭比比皆是。据说，开平有65万人口，在海外的乡亲则有75万之众。

闻名遐迩的碉楼，就记载着一个个华侨家庭或家族的兴衰，也维系着源于当地并延伸到世界各地的乡情和爱国传统。从最初到北美挖金矿、修铁路，到后来下南洋割胶开庄园，再到现在移居国外，碉楼见证了江门一代又一代人带着梦想开拓、跋涉的故事。

五邑的侨乡建筑，完全融合了西方建筑的特色，这其中，开平碉楼最为出名也最具特色。开平碉楼融合了中国传统乡村建筑文化与西方建筑文化的独特建筑艺术，成为中国华侨文化的纪念丰碑，体现了中国华侨与民众主动接受西方文化的历程。

开平碉楼的数量达到1800多座。2007年，“开平碉楼与村落”正式列入《世界遗产名录》，成为中国第35处世界遗产，中国由此诞生了首个华侨文化的世界遗产项目。

世界遗产委员会这样评价广东开平碉楼：是村落中修建

的一种具有防卫功能的多层塔楼式建筑。这些雕楼与周围的乡村景观和谐共存，体现了中西建筑结构和装饰形式复杂而绚丽的融合。

明朝以后，江门地区一度土匪猖獗，社会治安混乱。加上当地河流多，每遇台风暴雨，洪涝灾害频发，聪明的江门人选择在村中修建碉楼以求自保。

20世纪20年代，碉楼迎来修建的高峰期。在海外辛苦了几十年的华侨带上积蓄回到家乡，为了保护家人和财产安全，陆续建起以防盗功能为主的碉楼。

开平碉楼多是多层建筑，远高于一般的民居，便于居高临下防御；碉楼的墙体比普通的民居厚实坚固，不怕匪盗凿墙或火攻；碉楼的窗户比民居开口小，多有铁栅和窗扇，外设铁板窗门。碉楼上部的四角，一般都建有突出悬挑的全封闭或半封闭的角堡（俗称“燕子窝”），角堡内开设了向前和向下的射击孔，可以居高临下地还击进村之敌；同时，碉楼各层墙上开设有射击孔，增加了楼内居民的攻击点。

开平碉楼有不同的使用功能，也就有了不同的分类：众楼、居楼和更楼。

众楼建在村后，由全村人家或若干户人家集资共同兴建，每户分房一间，为临时躲避土匪或洪水使用。居楼也多建在村后，由富有人家独资建造，它结合防卫和居住两大功能，空间开敞，生活设施齐全。更楼主要建在村口或村外山冈、河岸，多配有探照灯和报警器，便于提前发现匪情，向各村预警。

开平碉楼的上部造型最具表现力，人们着力运用外国建筑中的穹顶、山花、柱式等建筑元素大做文章，形成了千楼千面的建筑式样。不同的建筑造型反映着楼主人的经济实力、审美情趣和受外来建筑文化影响的程度。

位于开平市塘口镇的自力村碉楼群是世界文化遗产地之一，因中国电影《让子弹飞》在此拍摄而名声大噪。《让子弹飞》是2010年上映的一部电影，讲述了北洋年间，南部中国一场惊天动地的火车劫案之后，号令山林的绿林悍匪张牧之，遭遇行走江湖的通天大骗老汤，两人从生死宿敌变成莫逆之交，然而真正的决战才刚刚开始，南国一霸黄四郎虎视眈眈镇守鹅城，一场场惊心动魄的决斗连环上演。

2017年，中国电影院的银幕总数已经超过4万块，成为世界上电影银幕最多的国家。中国电影似乎迎来了最好的时代，但真正深入人心的好电影却变得稀少。《让子弹飞》被认为是这个时代值得记录的电影之一。

《让子弹飞》的导演是姜文，同时也是主演。这是他的第四部电影，他是当代中国电影界的最重要人物之一。

云幻楼是自力村15座碉楼之一。1921年，占地面积80平方米的云幻楼建成。

这一年，中国仍在寻求独立富强之路。对中国人来说，这年最为重要的是中国共产党第一次全国代表大会在上海举行，中国共产党诞生。28年后，中国共产党成为中国的执政党，建立中华人民共和国。

云幻楼的建设者方文娴曾旅居马来西亚，热心公益。1918年，方文娴自捐5000元、募捐1.7万元回乡兴办强亚学校。日本侵华期间，他曾捐巨资支持抗日及购买自由公债。

为在家乡落叶归根，他建了这座碉楼。五层高的云幻楼，外部造型和装饰带有明显的西式风格。但在楼内，还保存着方文娴及家人使用过的生活用具，一派中国南方农村家居的传统形象。

他还亲自撰写楼联：云龙风虎际会常怀怎奈壮志莫愁只赢得湖海生涯空山岁月　幻影昙花身世如梦何妨豪情自放无负此阳春烟景大块文章。

对联表达的是：自己常有大干一番事业的愿望，可惜壮志难以实现，只能漂泊江湖，无奈蹉跎岁月；尽管一切皆是幻影，还是要抒发豪情，不能辜负了眼下如烟的春色、锦绣的文章。

在中国文化中，对联要有横批，这副对联的横批是：只谈风月。这位商人把自己爱国、爱乡的豪情壮志，及对动荡年代的愤懑和苦闷展示在对联中。

不仅仅是碉楼，在开平的乡间，就有一些村子，连村名也深深被打上了“侨”的印记，这些村子的出现和建设，就是一部缩影版的侨乡移民历史，其背后书写着侨乡人民艰苦奋斗的创业精神，以及对故国情深的爱国情怀。

提起侨村的建筑，让人感慨的是建造者在选材方面的讲究，奢华的房屋建造所需要的材料，有些是从海外直接采购。“加拿大村”雇请加拿大的设计师结合中西文化元素规划设计而成，并将村庄、别墅建设图纸从海外带回家乡依图而建。而建造别墅的钢筋、水泥和木头，也是加拿大华侨从加拿大运到香港，再由香港运回开平，来回一次需3个多月。

走进“缅甸村”，12间两层高的大屋分两行排列，整齐坐落在田野当中，而在村子前面则是空旷的地面，外面便是水塘。房子与房子之间的距离都是“等距离”，大概有2米宽，楼顶为硬山顶式瓦面结构，墙体为青砖结构，楼梯、楼阁大门均为柚木结构，横梁为“工”字铁外加柚木。

这些房子大部分是两房两廊一厅，小部分为一房一廊，而建房所需的柚木，从缅甸购进，而水泥、钢铁等，则从香港等地雇船运回。“缅甸村”的建设者是许遂兴，为了生计，他带着弟弟许纯兴远走他乡到缅甸，并在一家木材厂做起了杂工，因为勤奋努力，几年后，他们有了一定的积蓄，并办了一个名叫“万兴隆”的木板厂。鼎盛时，经营的店铺多达几十间，成为当地有名的商人。尽管在缅甸日子过得十分滋润，但许家两兄弟还是免不了对家乡的思念，于是他们后来回到家乡建房。

海外“发芽”根在江门

“爸爸去金山，快快要寄银，全家靠住你，有银好寄回。”这是首籍江门的华侨们熟悉的民谣。在旧中国，大量中国人被迫“卖猪仔”，漂洋过海到美国旧金山洗矿砂、做苦力，参与建造美国中央太平洋大铁路。建筑铁路的华工80%是江门人。太多人长眠在异国他乡。

一篇名为《浓浓侨情满江门》的文章介绍，孙中山领导辛亥革命，组建“兴中会”“同盟会”和国民党时，江门华侨都踊跃参加。孙中山组织了10次武装起义，所需经费多靠华侨支持，其中江门华侨贡献最大。他曾说“华侨为革命之母”，表明了海外华侨对革命极大的贡献。

1937年至1945年8月，江门华侨在美国捐款就达5600万美元以上。当时国民政府共发行6期救国公债，总额达30亿元，其中仅江门华侨就认购了11.1亿元。

2010年全面对外开放的江门五邑华侨华人博物馆，馆藏的4万余件华侨实物，全面忠实地记录了这段历史，展现五邑籍华侨华人在海外的艰辛创业以及回报家乡的感人故事。

台山斗山镇六村美唐村人陈宜禧，1844年生，11岁时赴美，后来参加美国铁路建设，成为铁路工程师。再后经商，经营“广德号”，参与了许多西雅图的承建工程，成为有影响的华商。美国排华期间，陈宜禧不畏强暴，为维护华人权益积极奔走，团结组织同胞奋勇抗争，受到侨胞的钦佩和爱戴，成为颇具影响力的侨领。

60岁时，陈宜禧放弃在美国优越的生活条件，回到贫困的家乡，带领乡亲集资建造一条属于中国人的铁路——新宁铁路。新宁铁路非但不借洋款，不收洋股，且不借洋工，自行修筑，从筹备、设计、修建、经营到管理都是由中国人独力完成，开风气之先。他决心要“以中国人之资本，筑中国人之铁路；以中国人之力量，创中国史之奇功！”

新宁铁路从1906年5月1日正式动工到1920年3月30日竣工，历时14年。铁路全长133公里，共有车站46个，桥梁215座，涵洞236个，并先后建成公益码头、北街码头、公益机器厂、牛湾船务等一大批工程，“转车盘”和轮渡火车更是中国铁路史上的创举，确立了以台城为交通枢纽、以新宁铁路为干线的水陆交通网络，成为民国时期江门五邑社会经济发展的大动脉。

1933年，巴金乘坐新宁铁路火车轮渡过潭江，写下了著名的散文《机器的诗》。

文中写道：“为了去看一个朋友，我做了一次新宁铁路上的旅客。我和三个朋友一路从会城到公益，我们坐在火车上大约坐三个钟头。时间长，天气热，但是我并不觉得寂寞。

南国的风物的确有一种迷人的力量。在我的眼里一切都显出一种梦境般的美：那样茂盛的绿树，那样明亮的红土，那一块一块的稻田，那一堆一堆的房屋，还有明镜似的河水，高耸的碉楼。南国的乡村，虽然里面包含了不少的痛苦，但是表面上它们还是很平静，很美丽的!到了潭江，火车停下来。车轮没有动，外面的景物却开始慢慢地移动了。这不是什么奇迹，这是新宁铁路上的一段最美丽的工程。”

新宁铁路前后经营30多年，抗战期间，遭到日军严重破坏，后被国民政府下令拆除，现仅存北街火车站旧址。

数据显示，祖籍江门的华侨、华人和港澳台同胞近400万人，遍布全球107个国家和地区，华侨、华人与市内人口基本相当，拥有“海内外两个江门”的说法。

美国原驻华大使骆家辉、美国旧金山市长李孟贤、美国奥克兰市长关丽珍、澳门特别行政区行政长官崔世安等政界人物，刘德华、周润发、谭咏麟、梁朝伟、甄子丹等香港演艺明星的祖籍都是江门。

华侨爱国爱乡，通过捐助公益、投资兴业等方式帮助家乡发展。截至2015年底，为家乡捐资捐物达72.6亿港元，回乡投资累计达201.2亿美元。江门特别设立“荣誉市民”授荣制度，以表彰在促进江门社会文明发展慈善公益事业、对外友好交往、经济科技建设等方面做出突出贡献的海外侨胞、外籍人士和国内人士。自1993年以来，先后共授予8批700位海内外人士“江门市荣誉市民”称号。

黄小娟就是“江门市荣誉市民”，她在马来西亚沙巴州长大，早年在加拿大求学。大学毕业后，跟随父亲做房地产生意，一步步成为沙巴著名的女企业家。

黄小娟的父亲黄国先后捐资百余万元，为台山当地学校修建操场、改造旧教学楼。黄小娟记得，1980年开始，父亲每年都要回老家探亲。1998年，首次到台山的黄小娟听说有小学需修缮，立即发动捐款。

对黄小娟来说，能成为江门和马来西亚沙巴两城之间经贸、文化往来的桥梁感到荣耀，对江门自己也有一种责任感。

祖籍江门的海外华人佼佼者中，应该还包括方美梅。1994年第36届格莱美音乐奖上，方美梅凭借《十个召唤者的故事》获得最佳音乐制作奖。这是华人第一次站在格莱美奖的领奖台上。

1964年出生于美国三藩市的方美梅，是第二代华人，祖籍广东省开平市塘口镇强亚村委会上塘村。她的父亲方创杰是当地著名的侨领，早在20世纪50年代已在三藩市创办了以自己名字命名的保险行。大学期间，方美梅就尝试影视制作，毕业后制作音乐录影片。

为了表彰方美梅所取得的成绩，三藩市市长办公室于1994年7月16日除了颁奖表扬方美梅外，还宣布16日为“方美梅日”。

图书在版编目（CIP）数据

活力的广东 / 徐静著．—广州：广东人民出版社，2017.6
（中国梦·广东故事）
ISBN 978-7-218-11890-1

Ⅰ.①活… Ⅱ.①徐… Ⅲ.①社会主义建设成就—广东 Ⅳ.①D619.65

中国版本图书馆CIP数据核字（2017）第128915号

HUOLI DE GUANGDONG
活力的广东 徐 静 著

出 版 人：肖风华

总 撰 稿：刘 旦
责任编辑：卢雪华 伍茗欣
封面设计：李桢涛
责任技编：周 杰 吴彦斌

出版发行：广东人民出版社
地 址：广州市大沙头四马路10号（邮政编码：510102）
电 话：（020）83798714（总编室）
传 真：（020）83780199
网 址：http://www. gdpph. com
印 刷：广东信源彩色印务有限公司
开 本：787mm×1092mm 1/32
印 张：6.5 **字 数**：200千
版 次：2017年6月第1版 2017年6月第1次印刷
定 价：60.00元

如发现印装质量问题，影响阅读，请与出版社（020-83795749）联系调换。
售书热线：（020）83795240